THE
GREEN
EDIT

HOME

EBURY
PRESS

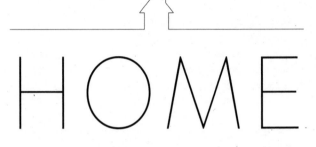

HOME

Easy tips for everyday sustainable living

KEZIA NEUSCH

CONTENTS

INTRODUCTION

Thank you for picking up this book. Maybe you are skimming through it while standing in a bustling shop, bringing it home as a gift for someone or working your way through the pages yourself …. Whichever person you are, thank you for wanting to look at your home and way of life in a new light. Welcome to a journey that may last the rest of your life, and one that I think you're going to love.

Now, a confession: I didn't find it easy to edit my home in a green way, but I did love every step and I wouldn't change a thing about what I did. More than creating a list of products to buy, things to do, or the different ways you need to cut down on or switch to new things, this process is about a shift in our mindsets. It's a process of letting go of some of the things you love, of considering how you could change the way you do things, then slowly finding new approaches that you might find you prefer to the old ways.

MY ZERO-WASTE JOURNEY

I have a close friend who was attempting to lead a zero-waste lifestyle long before it became a hashtag, and definitely before it had any hint of cool. Her goal was to create no rubbish in every area of her life – to put nothing in the bin and bring nothing into her home that had to leave again destined for landfill. Whenever she brought something into her home, she'd make sure she could either recycle it, compost it, or bury it in her garden at the end of its useful life. And, at first, I never quite understood it.

I suppose some part of me was intrigued and thought it was noble, but ultimately I thought she was choosing a hobby in life. I thought she just liked that way of living. One night, as we were making dinner together in her home, I scooped out a carton of sour cream into a bowl and found myself standing in her little kitchen holding the plastic container in my hand, not wanting to be caught. I looked around quickly: was there a bin?! What did I do with the carton? Did I need to take it away with me? I poked my head inside a cupboard ... 'You can put it in the box in there, for recycling.' Busted. She'd caught my clueless looks. I didn't think she was crazy, but – at the time – I thought that she definitely did things differently.

My own journey started from a different place. After having my first child, I was a stay-at-home mum, but also working – running a baking business from our tiny kitchen. One day, I stumbled through the front door, baby in tow, with the weekly food shop and plonked it all down on the kitchen table. Tired, I breathed out a done-for-another-week sigh, as I sat down and ignored putting it all away. And I just looked at it. It was a sea of plastic – so much so that I couldn't even see our food. Instead, I saw plastic around vegetables, plastic supporting food, plastic tying fruit together, plastic sealing things, plastic labelling things, plastic ... plastic ... everywhere.

"

I'd already read about the environmental damage caused by food being packaged in plastic and was starting to question its potential effect on our health.

"

I grew up in a home very focused on using food as a tool for health and I have always kept that value close to my heart. It led me to always choose food for myself and my family that was beneficial to our health in every way. I knew I had to make a change to how I shopped for food, but I also knew that we had a very rigid grocery budget to work with.

Honestly, the idea of reinventing our shopping habits in an economical way to what was, at the time, radically different to the habits we were used to, felt totally overwhelming. I wasn't ready to give up having a rubbish bin in my home.

When I was 12, my dad shared a fact with me that changed both of our lives. We were delving into the stash of chocolate that was kept in the high kitchen cupboard, out of reach. He told me about how much chocolate was likely made by slaves. I was shocked. That cupboard had held a secret story. That night, we agreed that we would never again buy or eat chocolate if we didn't know that it had come from somewhere where people were properly taken care of. It was one of my first interactions with thinking about how each thing that we bring into our homes has a story before it gets to us; and after it leaves us, too. I've turned down a lot of chocolate since then, and the decision to think about the before and after life of products has slowly led to changes in other areas of my life over the years.

It also brought home another truth to me: that I'm not entitled to everything in life. Chocolate is a luxury, not something that is truly 'needed'. I recognised that if our need for chocolate surpassed the importance of ensuring that people were not being exploited in the production of what was – for us – a treat, we really needed to shift our priorities and definition of 'needs'.

So, back in my kitchen, staring at that mountain of plastic, I took my first step towards making a change. Being greener doesn't happen at once, but we can all take a first step. I'd heard local people talk about a veggie box service, so I sat down with my laptop to find out what it was and sign up. I didn't really know what I was doing. Not getting to choose exactly which vegetables I would receive, and only getting what was in season felt a bit scary and completely out of my comfort zone. It was *certainly* not convenient. I mean, was it going to work for us, *or* work for our lower-than-average budget? I didn't know, but what I did know was that the plastic mountain wasn't working for us, and that this would be food with less plastic, fewer food miles and would have been saved from wastage, so it felt like a good place to start. A lot of my family's green journey has panned out like that – not really knowing if or how something is going to work but knowing that we were up for trying.

66

Sometimes things work, sometimes we have to find another route, but keeping it simple and having the freedom to express how we feel has helped us feel empowered to try things and make so many changes that all add up to a greener way of life.

99

Honestly, that veggie box took some adjusting to. We had to shape our lives a bit differently. It didn't come on the 'right' (read: easy) day for our schedule. It didn't always have the 'right' (read: what we were used to) foods in it. It didn't always leave room in our food budget for the other things we were accustomed to having. We had a choice: go back to plastic, find another way, or find a way forward with this veg box.

Even though it was inconvenient and a little more than we'd normally spend on produce, we knew we were moving away from making convenience our number one goal. Instead, we worked out what we could cut from the edges of our usual shop to make the numbers work. We found ways to eat more fruit and veg, so the extra spend in that area still fitted within our budget. We switched our usual meals around and found new things to cook. We worked out how to meal-plan with random veggies. Quickly, it began to feel normal and natural. I got into a routine of picking up the box, delving inside, letting the contents inspire a recipe, googling ingredients and what to do with them, shopping for the rest of what we needed, then using it all up.

Within just a few short months that scary box didn't seem complicated and unknown, inconvenient and abnormal. Pushing through the hurdles for what it *did* allow us to do, and finding new systems, was all we needed to make it our new normal. But you know what else became our new normal? Seeing less plastic. And as fresh produce without plastic started becoming normal, I started to notice the other things in our life that came in plastic and started to troubleshoot them, one by one.

As a new parent, I began to look at different options for baby clothes, baby products and nappies. Organic cotton, organic bamboo, cloth nappies made from organic fibres … I began to see the same issues that I had with food. And as I dug into plastic-free options for our health, I found a narrative about the environment as well. It hadn't been my motivation in life at all until that point. Aside from generally turning off lights, not littering and trying to get the right stuff into the recycling box, the welfare of the planet wasn't something I thought a lot about. But I'd begun to see our home in a different way, and I was starting to make different choices that, like the veggie box, weren't always the most convenient or natural for me.

Things that I'd never thought about before began to deeply hit my heart. I saw that the choices I was making in my own home went far beyond me. I knew I had a responsibility to the wider world to slow down and take more care over my decisions. Probably my biggest motivation when I was starting out was my children. I want them to soar in life, to have every option possible to them, and I don't want that next generation to have to exist to solve the problems that our generation created and perpetuated with our lifestyles. I don't want the choices that I make for *my* ease and convenience to cost *them* options in life. That is the only push I need when I'm hesitating to take the next step forward.

My other motivation is the realisation that how I behave towards the planet directly affects other people, not just in the future, but also right now. I don't want to live any part of my life at the expense of others. When I throw things in my bin, they might not affect my life anymore and they might have made my life easier, but they are going to

Don't get caught in thinking it's all going to be clear-cut: black and white, good and bad, a list of must-dos and must-nots.

landfill, they are decomposing, and they are having an effect on the planet that is adversely affecting people near and far. And that is why I keep going.

Don't get caught in thinking it's all going to be clear-cut: black and white, good and bad, a list of must-dos and must-nots. That just isn't true. Nor is this eco-friendly approach a productive mindset; it leads to a judgement of ourselves, judgement of others and the feeling that we'll never be able to make a difference. Ultimately, that undermines determination and hope – both of which are needed!

As humans, we are making footprints on this planet. These footprints show our use of resources and our effects – both positive and less positive. An actual human footprint on the ground can be measured by so many things: the shoe, the weight on the foot, the pattern, the pace or movement, the weather, the terrain. So, with life: we're all working with different things and we're all on a very personal journey. There isn't a 'one size fits all' approach.

We all leave footprints on this Earth, but I'd encourage you to look at it as thousands and thousands of little ones that you have power over each day. Every one of those can be made a little bit better – maybe not eradicated, but every move we make towards treading a little bit lighter, towards managing our lives and homes in a way that leaves a little less negative impact on the planet, matters.

What you're able to do today will be different from what

you're able to do tomorrow. What *I* can do will be different from what *you* can do. We all have different abilities, different resources and different limiting factors. It can be easy to look at our own personal position and set of defining factors and think about what we *can't* do with it. This book isn't going to tell you what you *should* be doing. It's not going to give you the perfect roadmap for your life and home. This book is going to guide you through discovering and assessing what you have to work with, then I hope it will help you understand what you could implement in your life, bit by bit, in a way that still feels like you and at a pace that works for you.

Remember:

- Slow change is often the most sustainable change.

- You're not always going to get it right (and that's ok).

- You *are* going to make a difference.

- You *are* going to adjust to new ways of doing things (I promise).

- You *are* going to find new ways of living that you actually love.

- You don't have to spend a lot of money doing it (unless you want to).

WORKING WITH WHAT WE DO HAVE

As my family has embarked on our journey of living a more sustainable life, people have told me that they feel guilty about what they can't do.

'I can't get to a store that sells food in bulk. I feel so bad that I have to buy it in plastic', for instance. One person told me that they had to take regular medications but were unhappy that there was no way to avoid the amount of plastic involved. In truth, most of us have some limiting factors and, while we can grow and learn, at the end of the day we can only be responsible for what we have the power to change. Usually the most lasting, sustainable changes are the ones we make because we *want* to, the ones we feel empowered to make, the ones we choose ourselves and truly implement into our lives in a way that works for us. From that place, one change leads to another, until slowly our lives look remarkably different from how they did before that first small step.

I know that some of the things I advise are just not accessible to everyone. I buy all my food plastic-free, but not everyone has a shop within an easy distance that sells food in that way. We all have different resources that can be used to take our best personal steps forward. Some people have time, some people have money, some people have certain skills, some have space and land, and some have access to certain ways of shopping. I want you to look at what you DO have and what you CAN give to this.

At this point, I'll let you into my secret confession: I *love* a good disposable sandwich bag. I love disposables in general – they keep life clean and simple, they save time and effort. So, you see, these changes haven't come naturally to me. Yet, I believe that, however slowly and imperfectly we did it, taking every step we could towards a healthier, more sustainable life was our only option. This is a fluid, personal journey. At one point or another, you're going to need to find your own conviction on why a greener way of living matters to you.

At points, the ease of staying in our comfort zones will try to pull us back from taking steps forward. In those moments, remembering why what we are trying to do matters is what keeps me from defaulting to a time-saving, money-saving, less-effortful path of least resistance. The reality of the world right now is that a life of treading a little lighter often feels like the path of *more* resistance. My hope is that, in this book, we can take an approach that feels manageable, that you can feel part of something – not alone – and connect to something a little deeper that helps to make the changes feel more natural and realistic in your own life.

This isn't a book about how to get it perfectly right. It is a book that will give you ideas, inspiration, encouragement and advice along your own personal journey.

GENERAL PRINCIPLES

CHAPTER 1

We all know that solving the problem is not going to be as easy as buying a book. In these pages I cover a wide range of ways to change our footprint and not all of them will be comfortable. For me, it was humbling to realise that people with far less than me often had a far less negative impact on the Earth. That people living, not necessarily through choice, in smaller spaces, with only the ability to walk as their mode of travel, only purchasing what they truly need and would use were, without even trying, creating a smaller negative footprint than me. It's important to remember that many of the steps I outline are in fact just an undoing of the huge amounts of waste that our comfortable and convenient ways of life have led us to create.

At the same time, this book should not make anyone feel judged for choices they have made before, and we should celebrate and value each little change that we make! Before we delve into more practical actions, there are some general mindset shifts we need to do which are foundational in helping to make the different decisions we need to take so that our homes can become kinder to the environment.

TWO SIDES TO CONVENIENCE

As I've said, at some point along the way in the journey to less waste everyone will get to the moment when it stops being convenient. This can be combated in different ways, and new norms can feel convenient again, but there is still a point at which we have to choose between convenience and our desire to create less waste or change our footprint.

Most of us have lives where some level of convenience is essential to maintaining our daily routine. But it's important to realise that there is more than one side to the convenience of so many of our daily practices. There is a slew of other 'costs' to convenient norms, other than the monetary costs that we've decided we're happy to pay. But that can mean it's an honestly painful and messy process when we come to release that convenience. I hope this book becomes a place where you can find new approaches that become convenient to you and feel just as easy as what you already know, but I also want to encourage you to reframe your thinking around convenience.

My point here is actually to make life feel easier, and remembering that there are two sides to the story can *help* in the moments when convenience threatens to slip into becoming the top factor again. There will be times when the extra inconvenience can feel tiring, or that striving to be better can feel overwhelming. The goal isn't perfection; you're going to do things that aren't perfect, or that you could have done differently, or that you might regret. The important thing is to try, to learn and to move forward.

SECOND-HAND
IS NOT
SECOND BEST

*It's funny how we've been conditioned
to think that new is better.*

Shiny, wrapped, fresh and new is often what we're taught
to love and value. Yet in some areas we do celebrate the
old: an item passed down through the generations, a
well-cared-for vintage car, an antique piece of furniture
or vintage clothing. We do have the capacity to love the
old. So why relegate second-hand items to second best?

Using and reusing the things that are already in existence
is one of the top ways to be eco-friendly in the home.
When something has already taken resources to be created, travelled miles, been packaged and ended up in my
home or close to me, that's the thing I want to turn to first.

66

Even if the new version of an
item has been produced ethically,
responsibly and/or sustainably,
the most eco-friendly choice is
often still second-hand.

99

Many people ask me how I feel when gifting second-hand items to my children. I've been asked if I feel bad or if they mind that they don't get new things. You know what? I feel GREAT gifting things with a lower footprint to my children and they love receiving them! I love knowing that their impact on the planet is less and also often on our finances, so we can afford to put money elsewhere which will benefit the children as well. But they also love it because they haven't been taught that it's second best. We celebrate used clothes, we get excited about buying second-hand toys and they don't see them as less valuable or less full of love, because they don't see *us* view them that way either. Whatever you're buying, you can apply the same attitude.

FAIL TO PLAN, PLAN TO FAIL

So many less eco-friendly decisions come out of a lack of planning and our need to move fast. One of the best ways to make more eco-friendly choices is simply to slow down on buying, plan ahead for what you need and make your peace with not needing things right away or finished so fast.

PLANNING MEALS

This lets you do things like soak dried beans and bake your own bread, which can save both a lot of packaging and resources. If you need an instant meal, it's harder to prepare food from dry ingredients or from scratch without planning ahead. To still get the convenience factor, make extra and pop the food in the freezer in portions, so you can pull them out as needed on a day when you are short of time. Cooking this way will usually save you money because you can buy ingredients in larger amounts, which can be cheaper. It can also have the added benefit of being more nutritious because you've cooked using fresh ingredients, rather than the kinds of things you can purchase that are ready to eat.

PLANNING EVENTS

Give yourself enough time to properly source what you need. Food is often a part of this and running to the shops for larger quantities of ready-made items can create a lot of waste. Planning ahead, even if it's not taking the time to make things, could let you think of easy-to-purchase or easy-to-borrow options that create less waste.

PLANNING GIFTS

Take a moment to really think about the person you are buying for in order to choose a thoughtful gift, but also to give yourself time to source something that's packaged the right way. Shopping for gifts at the last minute can lead to picking up much pricier choices, or just not finding what you need and having to go for a more wasteful option. Having some gifts always on hand (see page 152) has been really helpful for me, too.

PLANNING YOUR
WARDROBE

Being aware of your wardrobe, of what you do and don't have and what you specifically need, is a great help when trying to avoid fast-fashion purchases. You can slowly search out second-hand items, or watch for the sales of more eco-friendly companies, rather than suddenly needing an item and having to go wherever you can to get something, at whatever the cost.

WAIT BEFORE BUYING

In the age of clicking and having something arrive the next day, with seemingly no downside and at a low cost, too, it's easy to replace things the moment they break or when we feel the need for something new in our home. Giving up that need for instant gratification can give us a little space to feel what life is like without that item and make the best plan for replacing it. Before you do so, ask yourself if it could be fixed. It might take more effort or be more expensive, but where something can be mended, opt for that first. Then ask yourself if it's even a truly necessary item. We sometimes replace things just because we've always had them, without considering whether we really need them. Get creative: is there something else that could be used for the same purpose? After waiting and establishing that need, look at whether you can use an item that's already in circulation rather than buying new. Take the time to borrow or source something second-hand, if possible. Only once all of those options have been worked through should we look at buying a brand-new replacement.

LEARN TO ENJOY
WHAT YOU HAVE

Adding fewer items to your life and waiting longer for each thing you do acquire can make you appreciate what you have a lot more. If it didn't just come from the click of a button, if it was something you waited for, sought out and sourced well, it increases its value. And if you're finding yourself missing the acquisition of new stuff, take a look at who are you watching as you go on your journey. If instant home makeover shows and an Instagram feed of people shopping for new clothing items weekly are your normal viewing, it might be easier to switch off and seek out inspiration from people on the same sort of journey that you are on.

RETHINKING RESOURCES

Life creates a footprint, but rather than always being a negative term, it can be helpful to think of each of our lives as leaving a mark in so many different ways that can be both positive and negative. We are all leaving small footprints daily, with different impacts. If we only look at one big, negative footprint that we need to eradicate, even though this is needed, we are constantly fighting to get rid of something we can't fully remove from our lives. Trying to move towards something positive can be more inspiring than moving away from something negative. So, I think of my 'footprint' in a more holistic, fluid way.

The term 'zero waste' has tended to villainise all trash, which I think we need to step back from for a moment. That's not to say that filling our bins is ok, but that we should realise that not all rubbish is wasteful, and that not all wasteful practices result in rubbish. For example, rather than using a mug I already own, if I instead choose a compostable cup for my coffee, even though I might take it home and put it into my compost, I would still class that as waste. It's a wasteful use of resources and energy. Or if you already have a good-to-go plastic water bottle but see a new stainless-steel one rather than reusing one of the plastic ones you already own – that's wasteful too. It's an unnecessary use of resources.

So, perhaps we should be first looking at our resources, then designing our lives around them, not vice versa. This is a principle that is applicable to so many areas of

We all have a
footprint.

Not all rubbish
is waste.

Not all waste
is rubbish.

life – from food to clothing, to transport, to how we fill our homes. We are continually sold, in different ways, an idea of how our lives should look, the clothes we should be wearing, the food we should be eating, and so on. The problem with this increasingly globalised messaging is that it stops us looking at what we have available to us personally and shaping our lives around that. Instead of first looking at our own resources, it can be tempting to create a picture of what our life 'should' look like, then look at how to get it into our lives at any cost. This is when we start getting things shipped to us from far away in unnecessary packaging, things we don't truly need, things we could easily do without.

Instead, look at what is available to you and build your life from there. This might be very different to the next person, depending on where you live, and that is ok! Always look at what's produced locally, what's available second-hand, to rent or to borrow.

Going to an event? Can you borrow an outfit from a friend, or use one that you already have? Invite someone over who is a whiz with styling and ask them for help going through your wardrobe to find something suitable.

Cooking something up for dinner? First, look at what's available to you locally and in season, packaging-free, as a starting point. Don't look up a recipe then source the ingredients no matter the season, cost or packaging. Find local cooks on social media and look at what they are cooking for inspiration.

Looking to furnish your house? What can you find at shops in your neighbourhood that is made locally? Can you look at local second-hand sellers? What can you just live without? What can you repurpose?

It's a huge mindset shift and it goes against the grain, but it's the way we need to start thinking. The rush of buying the next 'in thing' or 'new thing' or 'colour of the season' or 'must-have' item is REAL! But I've found that the enjoyment I've experienced in items that I've slowed down for, written on my list and carefully sourced has actually been far greater and the appreciation ongoing.

"

The joy of value-led shopping and sourcing is a little bit deeper and can be financially beneficial and rewarding. It also carries the possibility of connecting you to the local community in a beautiful way.

"

BUDGETING FOR LOW WASTE

As the idea of living a low-waste lifestyle is becoming more mainstream, lots of companies have stepped up with products to help us eliminate common areas of waste in our lives. It's a wonderful thing to see solutions, but the flip side is a misconception that zero-waste living is about a perfect-looking, stainless-steel and aesthetically pleasing minimal lifestyle. If you start to believe that a low-waste life is primarily about curating collections of these eco products and alternatives, it can become a harder-to-attain and more expensive transition. It's maybe easier to consider them as peripherals to the central practices of a lower-waste lifestyle.

If you already have a plastic water bottle, keep on refilling it. Some people choose to move away from this low-waste option for health reasons associated with the potential effects of storing food and drink in plastic, but from a waste perspective, if you already own one it's a great place to start. Looking longer term, investing in a solid, long-lasting reusable water bottle is probably the most efficient move, but the cost is higher and you may not have space in your budget for it, so there's nothing wrong with using what you have and waiting to buy another one second-hand or when it is on sale. Even the speciality zero-waste products take energy to produce and often create some waste, so they too should be bought with care and a minimalist attitude.

A low-waste lifestyle needn't cost you more. There's no set way to reduce your waste; do what works for you, but don't feel that budget is an eliminating factor.

A lot of the waste we create actually comes from our ability to spend money, not our lack of money to spend on lowering our footprint.

Free and money-saving swaps

Lots of swaps that help us lower our waste are actually free or can save us money. I think these are great places to start, as they feel lower-risk and often more attainable. Here are a few ideas:

- **Turn off taps** So many of us aren't quite as quick as we could be at turning off the tap. Whether it's while we're brushing our teeth, running a bath, washing a plate, or while we apply shampoo or shave in the shower, trying to be one step more efficient in turning off taps whenever possible is a great way to save water and, depending on your situation, money on the water bill, too.

- **Turn off lights** Are you switching off lights as you move around the house or go out? Turning off lights (and any appliances you are not using) will save you money on your energy bill and use fewer resources. Some energy providers will provide customers with free energy meters so that you can monitor your usage.

- **Close the fridge** Lots of us are guilty of leaving the fridge open while we move something or grab something to put in it. Shutting the fridge or freezer door promptly, and only opening it when necessary reduces the power needed to bring it back to its set temperature.

- **Say no** One little word that can go so far! There are so many places where saying 'no' costs no money and reduces the use of resources. It's not always the easiest thing to say, I know that, but it's free and can make a massive difference. Say no thanks to a bottle of water in a meeting, to a takeout coffee, a bag in the shop ... think of where you can say no and save waste.

- **Don't buy coffee in to-go cups** How many paper cups get thrown away each day? Saying no to takeaway coffee in disposable cups is a fantastic way to save a lot of money and waste.

- **Take your own cup** It doesn't have to be a fancy new one – a mug from your home will often get you a discount and doesn't need to be an extra item that you have to buy.

- **Go paperless** It doesn't usually cost to go paperless with billing but it's an easy switch, saving on paper and the associated transport impact of the postal service.

- **Buy in bulk** Buying in larger amounts will save on packaging of lots of packets rather than just one, and it will be cheaper – even supermarkets offer a discount for buying something in bulk.

- **Make your own food at home** This is going to save on packaging, most likely save you money, and also gives you more control over the ingredients. You can buy ingredients in bulk or from better sources than they might come from when you eat food out. It lets you take exactly what you want rather than buying a portion that's too big or picking out and tossing away those tomatoes you don't like!

- **Buy dried beans** rather than canned. It's a small thing but it will be cheaper and save on packaging and the shipping of, basically, water. Even if you don't get package-free beans, the packaging on a kilo of dried beans is so much less than the tinned packaging on the equivalent amount of cooked beans. And much cheaper!

- **Make your own nut milk** If that's what you drink, making your own nut milk, even if you can't get nuts in bulk, will save a lot of packaging and food miles and you get control over the ingredients and quantity you make.

- **Use what you have** There are so many places, from food to clothing to furniture, where there's a temptation to buy new when really we can do so well using what we already have.

- **Shop during the sales** Don't be wooed by random purchases in the sales; instead keep an eye out for things you love. Keep a list of items you need to purchase in the near future and when it pops up at a discount, grab it.

- **Shop second-hand over new** Second-hand does not have to mean second best – see page 24.

- **Air-dry instead of using the tumble drier** Rather than using the energy required to run your tumble drier, simply hang up your clothes and sheets and open a window. It might take a little longer for them to dry, but the planet will thank you for it.

LOW-WASTE LIFESTYLE SPECIALITY PRODUCTS VS SIMPLE LOW-WASTE ALTERNATIVES

- **Stainless-steel water bottle**
  → A plastic water bottle you already have, or drink from a glass

- **Coffee- to-go mug**
  → A mug from home

- **Stainless-steel straw**
  → Save the last plastic straw you used and take care of it, or just drink from the cup!

- **Cleaning cloths/'unpaper' towels**
  → Cut up an old towel you don't need/want or have bought from a charity shop

- **Baby wipes**
  → Cut up an old T-shirt you don't need/want or have bought from a charity shop to use as reusable cloth

- **Cotton produce bags for a bulk shop**
  → Plastic bag, coffee bag, Ziploc bag, any container you already own

- **Pretty branded jute tote**
  → Old supermarket tote or repurposed bag you already own

- **Hair ties**
  → Chop up an old pair of tights or, if you see one in the street, pick it up and wash it well before use

- **Reusable coffee filters**
  → French press

- **Fancy on-the-go spork or utensil set**
  → A fork from home

LOCAL
RESOURCES

*The beauty of making changes to our lifestyles
to protect the planet in the twenty-first century
is that, increasingly, there are outside helping
hands – we're not alone.*

Some geographical areas are more ahead of the game,
but wherever you live it's worth digging into your local area
for support. Even if you think there's nothing, when you take
a closer look you may find that there are plenty of things
available to help you in different ways on your journey.

If you don't know of any local stores that can help you to
do bulk shopping or that offer low-waste options, a quick
online search for 'zero waste [enter your location]' or 'bulk
shops [enter location]' will help you find what might be
available in your area. Talking to other similar-minded
locals is usually the best way to learn, but you can also
look for people in your neighbourhood on social media
– it can be an amazing tool to find out what's available
near you. Likewise, if you find something great, let other
people know; create a community – it's so much easier
when you're not doing it alone! You can also look for local
groups that might give you community support.

Another thing to research is what recycling facilities are
available, either through regular recycling picked up from
your own address or at nearby locations. There might be options close to you that aren't kerbside, such as clothing and

shoe banks, or food drop-off points and community fridge set-ups. There are also more niche recycling points that will take things that aren't accepted in regular recycling set-ups, such as batteries or harder-to-recycle packaging. TerraCycle drop-off points can be found in some eco-friendly shops and are becoming more widely available.

Even if you don't have something directly available in your local area, more and more companies are providing long-range solutions. From bulk foods delivered to your door with returnable or compostable packaging, to doorstep milk or milk alternatives. The most widely available and most common doorstep option is probably some form of veg box. Local options will vary depending on where you live, but they can be a great starting point.

I'd also encourage anyone to think outside the box and go straight to the source whenever you can. Find out what is produced, grown or made locally and see if you can access it directly. Whether you're in the city or the country-side, you might be able to eliminate packaging, food miles and even some cost by going straight to the source. It might be local honey, a brewery, a bakery, a flour mill, or a farm for meat or eggs. Explore your local area and don't be afraid to ask questions. If nothing else, it will connect you to the local community, which often leads to finding other great things!

There are also more niche things you might find offered locally, such as a cloth nappy service or start-up set from your local authority; or swap and meet-up groups, which can be so helpful for resources and education. Sometimes local communities will have groups that go in together and rotate on driving to pick up and distribute items or veggie boxes from farms or producers, too. Just start asking and looking around your local area and you might be amazed what you find.

Using your local library is a great way to share resources and avoid buying new where you just don't need to. But the kinds of library you have available to you might be wider than just books. There are lots of things in life that can be shared between people. How about gardening tools? Clothes? Props? Cookware? Try looking in your local area for so-called 'Libraries of Things' or for what you can borrow instead of buy.

66

If you have a resource that you think could be used by others, consider making it available within a group that you're part of, or even starting your own lending library!

99

KERBSIDE RECYCLING

Kerbside recycling is a really helpful service that allows us to divert items from landfill and dispose of them correctly and easily. However, you do need to know how and what to put in your recycling bin. This will vary depending on where you are. For example, not all plastic is equal and different kinds can be recycled in different places. With a little research into your local area you may even find you're able to recycle more than you thought. Did you know some areas will offer pick-up for larger items or offer services for disposing of garden waste?

If you have a bin provided by your local authority there may be a note on it explaining how to recycle in your area, or if not look up your local authority's recycling rules online or contact them to get more information. Everything that goes into the bin has to be sorted, and placing the wrong items in there or not cleaning them correctly first can make the recycling process much more inefficient.

It is worth noting that the process of recycling uses up energy, too, and most items are not infinitely recyclable and will eventually end up in landfill. While it is better to recycle than throw something in the bin, the most eco-friendly option is, as always, to try and avoid packaging at all.

UNWANTED FOOD

There are more and more options popping up to eliminate the waste of unwanted but perfectly good food. There are a number of apps that can connect both restaurants and individuals who have food to give with people who need and want it, as well as foodbanks in your local area.

Community fridges are another option, and are becoming more widely available, offering places where locals can leave soon to expire food to avoid food waste. They also act as a food bank of sorts, providing access to fresh, nutritious food for people facing hardship.

GROW YOUR OWN

Growing some of your own reduces food miles and packaging, as well as being very satisfying.

While not everyone has the space for an allotment or full vegetable garden, even on the smallest patio or balcony, there's usually something that you can do.

If you do have outside space, growing things in a pot, in the ground, in a raised bed or even a bag, tub or hanging basket can all be great options. Ask a friend or look up local groups or blogs who may be able to tell you what grows well in your area and give you some advice about how to get started.

Even if you don't have any outside space, most people still have a windowsill and can grow something indoors. Look at what ingredients you tend to buy that come from the furthest distance or use the most packaging, then see if you can grow those plants in your home. Herbs are often a great option for growing in small pots in a sunny spot indoors.

You can even regrow some vegetables on a windowsill from the ends of used vegetable pieces! Spring onions, leeks, romaine lettuce and celery can all be regrown — simply keep the base part (the root end that is normally chopped off), place it root-end down in a glass of water and wait until you see regrowth. Once growing well, romaine can be transferred to a pot indoors. Herbs such as fresh coriander and basil can be placed in a glass of water until some roots appear, then planted out into a pot to grow on. You can even, with enough patience, regrow a pineapple in a small space and it can double as a pretty houseplant while it grows.

You could use your regrown plants as low-waste gifts. Charity shops often have a selection of plant pots for sale, and regrowing cut herbs or veggies in these and gifting them is a lovely idea. This sort of present not only creates no waste, it also benefits the planet and spreads the excitement of growing – indoors or out – to others.

KITCHEN

CHAPTER 2

EQUIPMENT

When putting together your green kitchen, you only need a minimal set of items, but do look for things that are built to last.

There are metal or wooden options available for most kitchen utensils, so invest in those and you will have a sustainable kit to last a lifetime (I say 'invest', but they're usually not expensive, especially if bought second-hand).

Look for sturdy utensils without plastic handles or component parts. Cast-iron and stainless-steel saucepans and casserole dishes (Dutch ovens) are close to indestructible and can easily be passed down through the generations, instead of those flimsier non-stick items that are more subject to wear and tear and often need replacing.

A single cast-iron frying pan/skillet is probably one of the most versatile kitchen items that you can have. It can be used for making pancakes, for slow-cooking stews, for mixing and baking cakes, crumbles and cookies, for boiling and steaming vegetables, frying steak, poaching, scrambling or frying eggs, and even for cooking bread and pizza. Because they last, they're also easy to find second-hand on online selling platforms, or in local flea markets or second-hand shops.

Other kitchen items to consider:

- Beeswax food wraps are a great replacement for cling-film and are fully compostable at the end of their life, you can also make your own if you're feeling like a project.

- Elasticated bowl covers are pieces of fabric that pop over the top of a bowl or container to semi-seal it. They're great for keeping food fresh, for covering proving bread and removing the need for clingfilm.

- Glass or stainless-steel containers to store food.

- Cotton or bamboo (or another natural fibre) cloths for cleaning, and natural-fibre cloths for drying washing-up and hands.

- A glass, refillable soap dispenser (you can also turn a jar into a reusable dispenser by buying just the pump parts, which are widely available).

- A reusable spray bottle for an all-purpose cleaner (see page 52) or other cleaners.

- Canning jars and old jam/pasta sauce jars for storage: glass jars can also serve as food containers for small amounts of food, homemade nut milk or leftovers.

- A scrubber made with more natural fibres, such as a wooden-handled brush with coconut-fibre bristles.

- Reusable silicon or fabric sandwich bags.

- Compostable baking parchment or reusable non-stick matting.

- Wooden and natural-fibre broom and stainless-steel dustpan.

- Natural-fibre mop head or reusable cover for a Swiffer-style mop, or just rags for cleaning a small floor space by hand. If you don't already own a handle, look for a well-made wooden or metal one that will last and avoid a plastic version or one that could break more easily.

- Metal or wooden drying rack for cutlery and dishes.

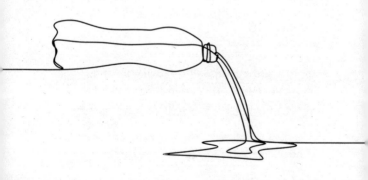

WATER USE

Anywhere there is a tap becomes a potential spot for wasting water. In the kitchen, putting a small sign by the tap can be a great way to start reducing the easily avoidable moments when people might not think and let the tap run. Something like 'Only use what you need!' will help you, partners, family and guests think about water use and turn the tap off a bit quicker.

Labelling glasses or using personal water bottles can also save lots of half cups getting wasted. This can be especially useful during a gathering. It not only saves on wasted beverages but also on washing up multiple glasses.

66

The more we train ourselves in the little areas that are avoidable, the more the idea instills itself and spreads and we become aware of our water use (or use of other resources) elsewhere.

99

COMPOSTING

There is a composting system out there for a wide range of homes, if you do some research. It's not just limited to people with large amounts of outdoor space. If you have a garden, you'll probably have the easiest time and the lowest costs, but if you're in a tiny apartment with no access to outside space you could freeze your compostables and take them to a local composting facility, farmers' market, or community-arranged compost system at no cost, and your local authority may have a weekly collection system in place, as well.

NATURAL CLEANING PRODUCTS

Cleaning products account for the accumulation of a lot of plastic bottles in the home. And not all of the ingredients in traditional cleaners are kind to the environment. There are three things I have in my cupboard with which I clean everything: liquid castile soap, bicarbonate of soda and white vinegar. Used in tandem with cut-up rags from old clothing or towels, natural biodegradable scrubbers and steel wool, they are just as effective as commercial products.

All-purpose vinegar cleaning spray is my number one product that I use to clean most things in our home. I fill a glass spray bottle with equal amounts of white vinegar and water, then I add a few drops of liquid castile soap. For added scent, I keep orange peels in a jar, pour over the vinegar, then let it stand for a few weeks before straining and using the vinegar to make a freshly scented cleaner. Alternatively, you can use a few drops of an essential oil as a natural fragrance. It does mean the house smells like vinegar when you clean, but it fades as it dries. I typically have two jars (old pasta jars or canning jars work well) on the go – one soaking orange peels and one ready to make my cleaning spray. I use the same spray without the castile soap to clean all the windows and glass in my home and wipe down with a T-shirt rag or towel.

Bicarbonate of soda is great for cleaning ovens. Apply it directly, leave for a few minutes and then rinse it off (I wipe it off with the above all-purpose spray). It's great to clean soap scum from baths and showers – simply touch a damp rag into the bicarbonate of soda and wipe down the mucky surface. It can also be used to clean sink drains; I sprinkle down a few tablespoons, let it sit for a minute or two (while I wipe down the surfaces!), then pour down warm water to rinse.

As well as cleaning, bicarbonate of soda is great for getting rid of smells – an open container of bicarbonate of soda in the fridge is probably a trick we're most familiar with, but those dish rags that have become a bit smelly can also be revived in a bowl of warm water with a few tablespoons of bicarbonate of soda dissolved in. And in the living room, sofas and rugs can get a little odour overhaul by sprinkling bicarbonate of soda (try using a fine sieve to spread it around) onto the fabric, let it sit for 15–30 minutes, then vacuum it up really well.

If making your own products doesn't feel like you, increasingly there are many shops springing up (both physical and online) where you can buy various ecological products in bulk, and to which you can take your own bottles and refill them to help to minimise waste. If you have to buy pre-packaged products, look for those with 'green' ingredients. I tend to look for those that are plant-based and have labels such as B corp, carbon neutral, compostable, organic, as well as being chlorine-free and fragrance-free, as a starting point. It's important to note that marketing can go a long way, so you do need to do some research into the company or the individual ingredients to be sure the product is as good as it claims to be. If something has a certification, that's usually a good sign, as it means the manufacturers are meeting some standards and it gives you something to research a little more. It takes more time initially to find something great, but once you do, you can repurchase it easily and it's worth the investigative effort. If you want to find something great with less personal effort, ask friends who you know shop this way, or in a local or online store with more Earth-friendly values to see what they stock.

CREATING A LOWER-FOOTPRINT CLEANING KIT

If you're putting together a new cleaning kit from scratch, here are a few things you could consider including:

- Glass spray bottles or recycled bottles with a spray top added on

- Natural rubber gloves

- Oxygen bleach

- Ecological dishwasher tablets

- Bamboo or natural-bristle brushes

- Compostable sponge cloths

- Coconut scourers and loofahs

- Ecological floor, toilet and bathroom scrubs

- Compostable bin bags, newspaper or waste paper to line bins

- Vinegar in bulk

- Bicarbonate of soda in bulk

- Plastic-free duster

- Rags – either purpose-made or use old clothes or bathroom towels

KITCHEN PAPER
ALTERNATIVES

Paper towels or kitchen paper are a large source of waste in many homes, but they're not a habit you need to eradicate – a switch to a reusable cloth instead of disposable ones can be a simple way to reduce waste. There are many other options for non-paper towels and some that even come wrapped around a holder like paper towels that can make the switch feel seamless and much easier. For a simpler, cheaper version, I take an old T-shirt and cut it into squares; they're great for wiping hands, for small spills, cleaning and so many other things. All these squares live on the work counter in a big glass jar so they're easily visible to us and guests who might be looking for a napkin or paper towel. Place an empty jar beside it or keep a bucket hidden under the sink for the used cloths. You can label the jars 'clean' and 'used', if you like.

For a lot of people, using paper towels is a habit, and cutting down on them can be really hard. You may find the easiest option is just to stop buying them. A regular kitchen cloth and a hand towel will deal with most situations where you would turn to a disposable towel. You don't actually need them!

RUBBISH BIN AUDIT

Call me crazy, but I want you to go through your rubbish!

If that sounds like one step too far, put paper and a pencil next to your bin and make a note of everything that you throw away for a week or two.

Your rubbish bin isn't the only place to assess your household waste, but it can shed light on your waste-creating practices and help you focus on the areas of life that need addressing. Lots of us (myself included) have become blind to the rubbish we create. We don't think about what we're putting in the bin or even recognise the waste-creating activities we're regularly engaging in because they seem so normal. A rubbish bin audit can be a great exercise to look at what you're throwing away, then you can work backwards to see if there are ways you can do things differently.

Once you've emptied those bin contents or completed your list, take a good hard look at what's there and ask yourself some questions:

SHOULD EVERYTHING IN THE BIN EVEN BE IN THERE?

For many of us, the bin is an easy place to put things we don't want to deal with or don't know where they should go. Rather than being a place to send a few unavoidable things to landfill, more often than not the bin has just become a place to declutter our house. I've seen people put all sorts in the bin: things they don't want to clean, items they don't want to repair, things they're done with or that they don't want to give away, clothes they don't want anymore, recyclable items they don't want to clean or separate out. The bin is just EASY.

This is mostly because we've lost touch with where rubbish goes and its effect on the planet. But it's important to stop viewing the bin as a magic black hole that makes things disappear. I'm very grateful for a system that means I don't have to bury the items I can't recycle or repurpose in my own garden, but I'm very aware that they are going somewhere and affecting our planet, even if once bin day comes I think I'll never feel the effects of them again.

I treat my
bin with
a healthy
respect and
gratitude, not
as a portal
to a cleaner
house.

SHOULD ANYTHING BE GOING INTO RECYCLING OR COMPOST?

IS THERE ANYTHING THAT REALLY SHOULD OR COULD BE REPURPOSED OR SAVED?

Sometimes, repurposing or saving isn't the easiest thing to do, but a greener lifestyle isn't always about what's easy. 'I don't want to save stuff, I just buy it when I need it.' 'Do I need to reuse an envelope? I prefer the look of a new one.' It's important to remember that you're re-writing your norms here, so you have to make some changes to get there. It might feel awkward or a little more work to start with, but it will become second nature in a very short time.

Not everyone can compost, but it's actually much more do-able than you think. Even if you don't home compost, most local authorities offer a composting scheme and will pick up your food waste for you. Depending on what composting system you have access to, different things are permitted to be included; if you're seeing veggie peelings and raw food scraps in your bin, dust from sweeping, hair and nail clippings or coffee grinds, all these could go into the compost.

After I sweep my floors, I take a moment to sort through what I've swept instead of putting it all in the bin. I take out anything that should be recycled or could be repurposed, such as bits of string. I'll usually take out a few stray pieces of plastic for the bin, and the rest can be composted.

Along with things that could go in the compost, look at whether there are any food items that actually could have been eaten. I want you to look at the food or produce that you throw away and ask yourself how you could have avoided that. Are there whole food items that went bad and didn't get used? Are you seeing common contenders? Are you always throwing away part of the loaf of bread or old bananas? Are there lunch-box items or kids' meals that just never get consumed? Do you faithfully buy certain items thinking you'll eat them, but it just doesn't happen?

Ask yourself what needs to change so that you either don't bring those extra items into your home or you use them when you do.

99

When you do find yourself with leftovers, see if there's a local place to drop or donate, or use the OLIO app or something similar to pass things on to someone who will use them. Work backwards and identify why things didn't get used and create an action plan to avoid getting to that point. Often it's just down to poor meal planning (see page 65).

HOW MUCH PLASTIC PACKAGING
COULD YOU REDUCE OR AVOID?

Take a look at the packaging on things you routinely buy and ask yourself how you could avoid that waste. Can you buy items in bulk to avoid throwing away lots of separate small packages? Are there other ways of buying your favourite produce that avoid using plastic? Could you cut down on your own consumption of those things? I found that cheese packaging was a frequent offender, so we now buy cheese from the deli counter – taking our own packaging and asking them to weigh it before it is added to the container.

4

IS THERE ANY 'GIFTED' RUBBISH?

There are always going to be areas that you can't fully control and you have to make your peace with that. As I looked through my own rubbish bag, I saw a good proportion of the rubbish was made up of things we hadn't chosen to bring into our home: the plastic wrapping from gifted flowers and food items, things other people had left after visiting, free gifts or party favours given to the kids when out and about. You can't always, but you may find that there are a few places where a polite 'no thank you' or a pre-emptive question when ordering something means you don't have to deal with that waste.

When out, ask questions like 'Does that come with any extras?' or 'Is there any plastic in that?' It's not convenient to remember to ask and sometimes I feel frustrated that it's on the customer to do so, but it sends a message that people care. It makes others feel as though they too can ask and say no, and it does reduce the amount that gets used and goes into the trash, either in my home or out and about.

Once you've completed your rubbish bin audit, take a look at your recycling bin. Are there any items in there that could come with less or no packaging?

FOOD WASTE

Food is one of the biggest creators of unneeded waste in the home – and it's a waste of resources at so many points along the chain – from the water and energy used in growing it, to transport and packaging, the energy used in storage, not to mention the financial cost. There are also factors after disposal to consider, as food doesn't break down in landfill the same way that it does in compost.

"

Food waste is a problem we really need to tackle, and by doing so it will probably save you money, too!

"

Do a regular fridge check

A regular assessment of your fridge contents is the best place to start. The fridge is where the items that deteriorate the quickest reside, so every 2–3 days check to see whether anything is going off. Think about the next few meals you have planned and whether you will use those items before they go bad. Then you have a couple of options:

- rejig your meal plan to incorporate those ingredients
- cook immediately and freeze
- freeze uncooked
- give it away

It sounds like a lot of work, but this kind of planning will soon become second nature. As you open the fridge to grab milk in the morning, spend 5 seconds looking over all the contents and thinking about what you can do with them, and you will find you can save so much waste.

Create a meal plan

Meal planning is a real game changer in helping to reduce food waste. Some people will plan only dinners, others will plan 21 meals a week, but whatever it looks like for you, buying food with a plan for how to use it in the time before it goes bad will transform your food-waste habits.

TIPS FOR LOW-WASTE MEAL PLANNING

- **Go through your calendar before you get planning and see what meals you'll actually need for the week ahead.** Consider whether you are cooking only for yourself or for the whole family, or whether you will have guests over or extra people for any meals. Take into account the needs of those people and plan accordingly.

- **Look at what foods are available to you locally, package-free or in minimal packaging, and build meal ideas around those ingredients.** This is more effective than starting with meal choices and then getting the ingredients in regardless.

- **Plan some 'leftovers' meals.** Leave some spaces in your meal plan where you don't decide on an actual recipe or buy ingredients for one. When it comes to that meal, only pull leftovers or things that need eating up from the fridge or cupboard and be creative. You can do this maybe once a week, depending on your routine. This will also encourage you to see leftovers from other meals as a potential new meal, rather than something to be tossed out. That extra cooked pasta that there wasn't enough sauce for on pasta night? Save it for leftover night and get creative – add some cheese, or just butter and seasoning, or another leftover item that might work to create a new meal.

- **Remember that not all meals need a 'name'.** This is a massive mindset shift for many people. Meals can just be foods put together in a way that works for you! You don't have to create a named dish and follow a recipe to the letter. Look up an ingredient online for ideas of how it can be cooked or prepared and work with that and whatever else you have to put together your own meal. If you do have a random selection of leftover ingredients and you just don't know how to use them, pop 'recipe [insert a few ingredient names]' into an internet search engine and choose one that best fits what you have.

ENTERTAINING

Entertaining guests might need to be a bit different from what you're used to, but that's ok!

Finding staple ways to do the kind of entertaining that works for you is going to be key.

- If you love to cook, find go-to recipes that are great for a crowd and which utilise ingredients that create less waste in your life, then rotate them.

- Let guests know that there are alternatives to some of the things they might expect to find in your house and let them know how they work, so they don't feel alienated or judged for not knowing, especially if they are in your home for a length of time. Let them know how your composting system works, or what they can use instead of a paper towel or napkin, or plastic straw.

- Don't use these moments to educate or give someone a lecture about why your way is better, just use it as an opportunity to show them how you live and make them feel comfortable about how you do things. Seeing how easy it is to make the swaps might make them consider making their own switches more effectively than being given a pep talk.

- Be confident about the switches you are making, don't hide them or feel bad about them. You are powerful and you choose to do these things for a reason you believe in!

- If you don't have enough plates or cutlery for a crowd, look at buying extras at a second-hand store, borrow some from friends or neighbours, or have guests bring their own to the gathering, so you don't need to use disposables.

- Invest in enough cloth napkins or, if you have lots of people or lots of kids around, pull out that jar of cut-up T-shirts and share them out. When you're clearing up the table, show people where the dirty cloths go.

DIY *waste savers*

Not everyone wants to make their own food at home, but sometimes it's less work than you might think. If your goal is to bring less packaging into your home, creating some dishes from scratch can be a great way to do it. Look at the recipes that create the most waste in your kitchen and try to make them yourself instead. Alternatively, look at the things that feel the easiest to make yourself and start there.

Creating your own meals from scratch often saves money, but the actual reduction in waste will depend on whether you are able to get the basic ingredients packaging-free, or at least packaged better than the final ready-made product.

- **Baking your own bread** Making your own bread is one of the best places to start (see recipe on page 72). It is almost always cheaper to make bread at home than to buy a loaf of the same quality, and it doesn't need to be a painstaking process. Flour is something that most people can purchase plastic-free, as mostly it is packaged in paper, so it's a great place to start. Find a recipe that works for you. For the cheapest and lowest-waste option that doesn't even require you to buy yeast, try making your own sourdough starter, or get a little from someone else's. Many bakeries will give away some of their starter if you ask nicely. If you have space to store it, you might be able to buy large sacks of flour in bulk.

- **Kids' food** One of the biggest complaints I hear about baby-led weaning is the mess and food wastage it creates. This can be avoided by putting food on a big plate in the centre of the table, then loading up kids' plates slowly as they eat, rather than filling their plates and being left with a lot of mauled leftovers or food on the floor. It drastically reduces the amount of wastage and mess.

- **Buffet-style eating** The help-yourself concept works at any age. Especially when we have guests, I tend to let people serve themselves. It's not as elegant as serving plated food, but it means that every person can judge for themselves how much they need or want to eat. They help themselves if they need more and they can leave something off their plate if they don't like it. Serving smaller portions across the board is a good way to accomplish the same thing if you're finding there is often food left on plates.

- **Eliminate snacking** This has really helped us reduce food waste at the table, as the kids (and all of us!) arrive hungry and ready to eat at mealtimes. This way we don't reject items or are picky, so the food we've cooked actually gets eaten. *Bonus:* it also reduces costs, as snack foods can often be quite expensive, and it reduces packaging waste as snacks are often more heavily packaged in individual wrappings.

Waste-saving recipes

OUR GO-TO BREAD RECIPE
[MAKES 1 LOAF]

Baking your own bread can seem intimidating – what with the kneading, rising and proving involved – but with a simple recipe it can be a source of low-waste, budget-friendly joy! Plus it will make your kitchen smell incredible. You can easily double the recipe then slice and freeze one loaf, so the work is done for another day. (I re-use an old bread bag, use a silicon reusable bag, or wrap it in a cotton tea towel and freeze it just wrapped like that.) There are many different methods for making loaves of bread but this is our easy everyday method that we – and many others – have been using for years.

INGREDIENTS:

- 400g/14oz/3 cups wholegrain flour, plus extra for dusting
- 1 teaspoon salt
- 1 tablespoon dried active yeast

- 230–350ml/8–12fl oz/ 1–1½ cups warm water
- vegetable oil or butter, for greasing the tin (optional)

METHOD:

1. For this recipe I use a 450g/1lb loaf tin, but I've baked it in many vessels and you can absolutely work with what you have. A larger bread tin will yield a slightly shorter loaf. You can also use a casserole dish/Dutch oven, or bake it shaped in a ball on a baking sheet – it won't reach the same height, as the sides of the tin give it shape, but it will still make delicious bread.

2. Put the flour, salt and yeast into a large mixing bowl and thoroughly mix together with a spoon. Slowly add the water, mixing until it comes together in a sticky ball of dough. You may not need all the water.

3. Tip the dough out onto a well-floured work surface and knead (folding the edges into the centre and pressing down, then rotating, pulling in another edge and pressing down) for 5–10 minutes, until the dough is stretchy and smooth.

4. Place the dough in a lined (I suggest using compostable baking parchment, which can be reused for many rounds of baking) or oiled loaf tin, cover with a damp tea towel and place in a warm place for about 1 hour, or until the dough has doubled in size.

5. Meanwhile, heat the oven to 150°C/300°F/gas mark 2.

6. Bake the loaf for 35 minutes, or until the bottom gives a hollow sound when tapped.

7. Tip out of the tin and cool on a wire rack.

PIZZA

[MAKES 2 10" PIZZAS]

The same bread dough recipe also makes a great pizza crust, which is a really delicious way to use up little bits of leftovers from the fridge or freezer. Small amounts of meat, beans, pesto, tomato sauce, extra veggies and ends of cheese come together in a really easy meal. You don't need to use traditional mozzarella cheese, just add whatever you have – or leave the cheese out altogether.

METHOD:

1. Follow the bread recipe to the end of step 3. Place the dough in a lightly oiled bowl and cover with a damp tea towel or beeswax wrap for 1–2 hours until it has doubled in size. Heat the oven to 200°C/400°F/gas mark 6.

2. Divide the dough in half. On a lightly floured work surface, roll it out to a round with a rolling pin or press it out with your fingers. Heat a cast-iron frying pan/skillet over a high heat until it's hot, then carefully place the dough onto the hot pan and load it up with your toppings. Transfer the hot pan to the oven and bake for 10 minutes, or until the cheese is bubbly and beginning to brown.

3. Repeat to make a second pizza.

4. You can also do this on a baking sheet. Put the naked dough base into the oven to bake for 5 minutes, then remove from the oven and carefully add the toppings. Return to the oven and bake for a further 10 minutes, or until the cheese is melted and just beginning to brown.

If your goal is to bring less packaging into your home, creating some dishes from scratch can be a great way to do it.

MORE TIPS FOR USING UP LEFTOVERS

There are plenty of ways in which you can use all those bits and bobs of leftovers hanging around in your fridge to make delicious dishes:

- **Save bits of fruits and veg in the freezer** So many things that might be put in the bin or the compost can actually still be used. If I don't have an immediate use for leftover or old bits of fruit and veg, I pop them in the freezer. I keep a sweet bowl and a savoury bowl, which I use as 'ready-for-smoothies' and 'ready-for-soup/stock'. Then, whenever I make the next batch of one of those things, I reach for the freezer stash first and finish them off with fresh or new ingredients.

- **Smoothies** These drinks can pull together so many odds and ends into a delicious whole. Fruits that might be less pretty, certain veggies, nut and seed butters, nuts and seeds themselves, milk, yogurt, juice ... There's no set way to make a smoothie!

- **Soup** This is a great vessel for using up ends of things. Those ingredients that tend to sit at the bottom of the fridge can often be diced, cooked and added to a blender to create soup. Look up recipes if you need inspiration – you can find soups to which you can add leftover pasta or beans, too, then serve it with toasted older bread, or use stale bread to make some croutons for the top.

- **Tacos** Another great way of using a bunch of leftover 'bits' to make a brand new meal. Simply throw them in and wrap them up. You could make your own tacos, buy them, or use whole lettuce leaves as a wrap.

- **Veggie hash with eggs** Lots of those veggies that might sit in the bottom of your fridge (think carrots, onions, courgettes, mushrooms) can make a great veggie hash. Dice them and either pan-fry until they're soft on the inside and getting charred on the outside, or toss them in oil and salt and bake in the oven at a high heat until they're soft and nicely cooked but crispy on the outside. Add in leftover chopped herbs, too, for flavour. Serve with a fried egg on top or leave it off for a totally plant-based meal.

- **Curry** Keep a jar of curry sauce on hand or make your own. A good way to use up leftover meat and veg is to add a sauce that pulls everything together with great flavour. Make a meat one or a veggie one, adding in whatever you have. Serve with rice or bread or whatever grains or sides you have on hand.

- **Leftover bread** The statistics on the amount of bread that gets wasted are close to unbelievable. Think how often the end slice gets thrown out, or some of a loaf gets forgotten about and goes mouldy. Slicing bread and storing it in the freezer can be a great way to prevent it getting to this point, but if you do end up with slightly stale bread, try toasting it, using it for French toast or croutons, or turning it into homemade breadcrumbs. Just blitz stale dry bread in a blender or grate it on a grater and store in a dry, well-sealed container. It will keep well for two months in the freezer. Then just work something that needs breadcrumbs into your meal plan. I often mix them with a little grated cheese and put them on top of mac 'n' cheese for a crispy crust. It's delicious! Bonus – it saves on the waste packaging of buying breadcrumbs when you need them.

- **Use ice-cube trays to freeze food** Freeze small amounts of food in ice-cube trays to use as needed – such as stock, milk, juice, or butter with herbs in it. Not only is it a great tool for preserving things that might go bad, but it works well for where you only want a small amount of the item. Maybe you have milk in your coffee but only a few times a week. Chopped herbs can be mixed with small amounts of butter, oil or water, and frozen to keep them fresh. I also use ice-cube trays for saving the ends of a smoothie if we don't drink all of it. Then, when we make another one, I can throw those cubes in too. If you're looking to invest in a plastic-free option for ice-cube trays, there are stainless-steel ones out there.

Weigh your coffee!

I noticed that when we brewed coffee, we were often either leaving some behind in the French press or in our cups. A quick calculation showed me just how much money we were throwing away in coffee and how much waste we were creating. In addition to the wasted coffee beans, there was the extra water that wasn't needed to brew the extra coffee and the wasted energy used to heat that water. There was also the indirect wastage of growing that unused coffee, of packaging it and transporting it – it all added up. I decided we would weigh it to get it right every time and only use the amount we needed.

Try to think about the amount of water you need and only add that to the kettle, to save wasting energy on boiling water you don't need. Use a bit of planning and only boil water when you're making the coffee. It's easy to put the kettle on, then forget and come back and reboil – and that all uses up energy that could be saved! Zero-waste coffee isn't just about not putting something in the bin at the end of the process.

To brew coffee, a stainless-steel French press is the simplest and least wasteful solution. It requires no paper filter as the grinds go into the press and that's it. You can also control the number of cups you make at a time. Then the used grinds can go into the compost, meaning nothing goes to landfill.

In terms of coffee packaging, if you can buy coffee in bulk, that's going to eliminate a significant amount of packaging waste. At bulk stores, coffee is often one of the options provided, and some coffee shops and roasters will let you bring your own packaging to bulk buy.

Otherwise, opt either for compostable packaging (which, again, is becoming more easy to find) or the largest container you can find.

Lastly, take note: do you usually finish your coffee or leave a bit? If you're routinely cleaning cups with coffee left in them, consider adjusting the amount you make (see above), or consider saving it to reheat or make an iced coffee later in the day, or even the next day.

66

> We can take a lesson from this process, as so many areas of life can be run through the same filter.
>
> Are you taking more than you need? Can you hone in on simple ways to make things more sustainable? And what, for you, is the next step forward in lowering the waste surrounding any given activity?

99

HOW TO DO
A LOW-WASTE
FOOD SHOP

We can grow our own food, we can shop in bulk, we can go straight to farmers' markets or farm shops, but what if you just want to buy your groceries in a regular supermarket or neighbourhood shop and still aim for a lower footprint?

Note: If you have the time and you're going to be shopping at a particular shop in the long term, see if you can walk round before you make your meal plan and familiarise yourself with the products. Look at what is sold package-free, what is packaged in paper, and what the prices are on those items. Build your meal plans with that knowledge in mind and it really helps with reducing your footprint.

Good shopping starts before you even leave the house:

1. Make a meal plan and use it to write a shopping list. This helps you to avoid buying food you don't need, saving on food waste before you even start shopping.

2. Grab your reusable bags and smaller produce bags for fruits and veg.

3. Consider how you will travel to and from the shops. If you need to use a car, can you do a larger shop to reduce journeys and save fuel? Can you go with someone and do your shopping trip together?

4. When you get to the shops, try to remember why you do what you do. Remember that convenience and momentary personal 'wants' might not need to be your top motivators.

As you shop, remember all the things that create a footprint before (and after) the items get into your basket. It's an area you can get deeper and deeper into, but don't get overwhelmed, start where you can! The easiest place to begin is looking at packaging.

5. Shop for produce that is sold loose – namely, fruit and vegetables – as much as possible. Try to create your meal plans around those items, if you can.

6. Moving on to packaged items, remember that bigger packages equate to less packaging per serving. Look at what things are made of; single-use plastic is the biggest no-no, but what if it's impossible to avoid? My advice is to look at your usage: sometimes there will be plastic-wrapped products you buy every single week and sometimes ones that contain many months' worth of servings, so over time they represent a smaller amount of plastic. Work hardest on eliminating from your life the items you need to buy most often.

7. Look at whether the packaging is made from a type of plastic that can be recycled in your area. Sometimes different brands of the same product use different kinds of plastic. Prioritise the types that you know you can recycle.

8. Paper or card packaging might already be recycled, or it might be new; it might come from responsible sources, or it might not. Environmentally responsible brands will usually clearly highlight this on their packaging, so look out for those claims. Check to see if it is paper that can be recycled or composted; sometimes packaging products can look like paper but be coated or combined with other materials that make them much harder or impossible to recycle (such as disposable coffee cups).

9. Compostable packaging is an option that is increasingly showing up in all areas of life. There are a few points to consider here: 'compostable' can mean different things, it's not something that just happens to a product, it's reliant on a specific set of conditions to make that process occur. You don't want your coffee cup to disintegrate as you use it, but you do want it to eventually break down in the compost. But it means that if you don't have access to these specific conditions, you don't get the celebrated results. Just like food doesn't break down the way most people expect it to in landfill, different materials need different conditions to actually live out the 'compostable' claims. The biggest things to look for are whether something is commercially compostable or home compostable. If an item is home compostable, it will still need to go into a home compost heap to reap those benefits; if something is commercially compostable, you'll need to have access to a commercial composting facility to see that happen.

Just remember, compostable packaging still uses up resources and energy. Don't shift a single-use mindset over to compostables. We need to stop prioritising convenience as key, otherwise we'll just look for different ways to fulfill that need for convenience instead of building new systems. That said, if you have to choose one kind of packaging over another and you have the ability to dispose of it correctly, compostable is a great way forward.

10. Consider food miles. Look at where your products come from. There are multiple reasons for doing this, but the major one is how many miles your food has travelled and how much fuel was used to bring it, contributing to its carbon footprint. Start to become familiar with what foods are grown closer to home and see if you can make shifts towards consuming these items. Even the variety of apple you choose might mean the difference between food transported from the other side of the world to food grown more locally.

11. Constantly question yourself about the level of need you have for an item versus the potential environmental cost. For luxury items, you might want to set higher standards and have less room for compromise on packaging. For essential items, while you should still look for the best on every aspect of it, you might not be able to go without just because there isn't a good option.

INTERIOR DÉCOR

CHAPTER 3

REDECORATING YOUR HOME

Redecorating, upcycling and interior projects are all areas where we bring pre-loved things into our homes as a new object without having to buy an item that's 'new'.

When obtaining materials for any home project we want to really think about where the items came from, how their production has impacted the environment and how they'll be disposed of when they come to the end of their useful life. From fabrics to glues to other materials, there are small steps we can take to make better choices.

For fabrics, I love deadstock fabrics that would otherwise go to waste. Even if they're not perfect in and of themselves, saving something from potentially going to landfill that's already in circulation is a great option for me. If you ask a local fabric store they may be able to give you unused or old pieces for projects. When I'm looking for new fabrics, the first place that I start is with natural materials, as I think about both their end of life and creation. Then I look for organically grown and more sustainable options, and more natural dyes or undyed fabrics. I'd say dyes like fibre-reactive and vegetable dyes can be better options, but ask questions and look for a company's efforts to use more eco-friendly methods.

FURNITURE

When it comes to furniture, there are a lot of potentially complex things to consider and, being larger-ticket items, price really comes into play here for most people. The simplest way to reduce our environmental impact in this case is to keep it simple and use what furniture there is already in circulation.

66

It might mean you have to adapt the look you're going for, but you can make a huge impact by not buying new.

99

You can source used items from many places. Consider local charity shops that carry large furniture, social-media selling platforms, dedicated online selling sites (such as Gumtree), garage and car-boot sales, flea markets, second-hand fairs, or even at auction. For a less hand-me-down feel, there are also gems to be found in antique shops, vintage and second-hand shops – upcycling companies can also be a fun way to get something unique but partially used. You could also look at upcycling what you already have or an item that you can find second-hand. There are plenty of inspiration and tutorials to be found online.

If you have no other option but to buy new, look at where the item is made, the materials used and how they were sourced. Choose materials such as metal and wood, and consider the fixtures and other component parts, trying to avoid plastic where possible. Wooden furniture tends to be the easiest to repair if things break, and metal tends to be sturdier than plastic and so lasts longer. Look for natural-fibre fabrics that were organically grown and sustainably sourced.

Think about wear and tear, too. This will affect the lifespan of an item, which in turn impacts the waste you could potentially create. Ideally, you want things to last a lifetime. Ask yourself:

- Can it be washed, or will it be easy to clean?

- Is it in a colour that's going to be long lasting across time and seasons?

- Is it a timeless style rather than just the in-thing right now?

- Is it adaptable – will it work in different rooms, in different seasons and with numerous décor styles?

- Is it sturdy and well made – will it stand up to wear and tear over time?

HOUSEPLANTS

Placing plants around your home can be a great way to decorate and change things up seasonally in a very natural way, but they also have so many other benefits worth noting. Plants both help clean particles out of the air and reoxygenate it, and are also said to act as filters to trap allergens and take in potentially harmful volatile organic compounds (VOCs) and return the humidity to the air that is removed by air conditioners.

Bought plants often come in plastic pots, but if you find you have lots of them left over after planting out or re-potting, you may be able to return them to a garden centre or donate them to other gardeners. Alternatively, use them yourself to grow some new plants from seed – maybe some herbs (see page 44).

Use water that might otherwise go straight down the drain to water your plants. Those half-drunk glasses of water that get left to go stale? Pour them into your plant pots. If you need to run the tap for a while before your hot water kicks in, put a bucket or jug under it and collect the water to use on your plants – inside or outside.

And maybe at Christmas, instead of buying a Christmas tree you could decorate a houseplant!

NATURAL HOME SCENTS AND CANDLES

There are many ways to freshen a home or bring nice scents into a room that are really eco-friendly. Here's a list of just some of my favourites.

- Scented candles are a fragrant favourite – look for refillable, reusable or recyclable options, with no additional packaging. There are a few other environmentally-unfriendly traps here, such as what the wax, wick and scent are all made from. Depending on where you are, a locally produced option is probably best to reduce carbon footprint and many farmers' markets will have very local beeswax candles available for sale. You could even experiment with making your own candles with local beeswax. When looking at wicks, look for those that don't have a metal base and instead use just simple cotton, wood or hemp.

- Heat essential oils in a ceramic diffuser or pan using sustainably sourced oils. Or add these to your vinegar cleaning spray for a little fragrance. Sprinkle dryer balls with a few drops of essential oil to give sheets and towels a home freshness.

- Simmer cinnamon powder or a few drops of an essential oil on the hob.

- Baking bread is an amazing way to make your house smell warm and inviting.

- Eucalyptus in the shower.

"

Keeping the house clean will
keep odours at bay, and whenever
possible, throw the windows open
to clear the air.

"

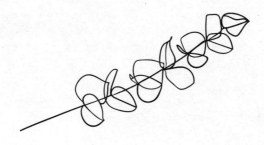

SEASONAL
DÉCOR

*Festive celebrations like Christmas, Easter
and Halloween are times when a lot of extra
decorations can enter our homes that are often
plastic, single-use or disposable.*

If you're used to decorating in this way it can feel hard to
let go of the habit, but I'd encourage you to embrace new
family traditions and ways of celebrating the seasons that
are more gentle towards the Earth. Making your own decorations or buying simpler items can have added benefits,
like being easier on the wallet, providing fun activities for
the family in school holidays at those times of year, or
even being potentially better for our health by bringing
more natural items into our homes.

- **Rather than putting out plastic pumpkins at Hallow-een, use real pumpkins.** If you are scooping out the middles to use them as lanterns, keep the flesh and the seeds and use them both in delicious recipes. Or if you prefer, you can decorate the home with whole fresh pumpkins, then use them up before they go bad. Once you've taken what you need from the pumpkins, you can compost the rest.

- **Decorate your home with things you can find in nature.** Fruits and leaves can be used for table centre-pieces or garlands, then composted afterwards.

- **Use recycled paper and paper tape or a water and flour glue to make paper chains, pinatas and other decorative items.**

- **Look in second-hand shops for decorations or find new ways to use what you already own.**

- **Look for Easter eggs and other edible seasonal items that are sold only in packaging that's recyclable in your local area or compostable.** There are lots of widely available options! Also look into the provenance of the chocolate, making sure you only buy that which has been fairly traded.

- **For Easter egg hunts, hide the actual chocolate eggs rather than a plastic alternative, or use real hard-boiled eggs.** And if you look around your house you'll likely find lots of things that could be used as a basket.

- **There are lots of options for Christmas trees.** Obviously, not getting a tree at all (whether real or artificial) has the lowest footprint, or you can forage for a branch that you can decorate – they can make stunning alternative 'trees'!

  - If you already have an artificial tree, or if you have access to a second-hand one, continue to use it and take good care of it to keep it going for as long as possible.

  - Try a more sustainable artificial tree alternative, such as ones made of wood or fabric that can be decorated and kept year on year.

  - If you can, source a real tree that's grown locally and organically. This reduces the transportation footprint and helps support local businesses.

  - Buy a potted tree that you can plant or keep outside and bring inside each year. There are also lots of schemes that allow you to hire a tree, returning it to the company to be planted out and cared for during the year, then re-hired the following Christmas.

  - Make sure you dispose of a real Christmas tree properly, either through local schemes or by composting.

- **If you tend to put up strings of fairy lights during the winter and leave them there for months, consider at other times if you really need them on and switch them off at night or whenever you can.** It can feel easier to buy a new string when one light goes out, but if you save the spare bulbs they tend to come with you can replace them and extend the life of the lights.

- **Christmas crackers** are usually a disposable decorative table accessory with items inside that get tossed fairly quickly. Look for reusable ones or recyclable ones with thoughtful, eco-friendly gifts inside, or consider making your own so you can make them perfect for your table.

- **Party bags, Easter baskets and Christmas stockings** – these small-item collections of low-cost gifts are often places where huge amounts of small disposable items come in to play. The thing I find most helpful in avoiding this is to set a reminder in my calendar a few months before these events and then be on the lookout for small things when I find them or take the time to source them to my values. Set a reminder in advance of Easter, Christmas, children's birthday parties or other times when you're creating these collections of little gifts so you can prepare more mindful options.

BATHROOM

CHAPTER 4

Consider what you really need, use up what you have and simplify

The bathroom is a place where we often use and accumulate a large number of bottles, tubes, etc. For lots of people, the switch to using products that are safer for the environment ties in to a quest for finding those that are safer for human health. A lot of the companies that use less-harmful ingredients are also the ones making efforts to be more sustainable, so there is often a lot of overlap in these areas. Don't feel you have to switch everything out at once, instead, as you use something up, look for a greener alternative to replace it with.

As a starting point, look for products that use less packaging. There are lots of things – like bar soap, that don't necessarily need packaging, so these are easier to buy loose. For items that do come pre-packaged, look for those wrapped in natural materials, that can be recycled or composted, or that have already been recycled. Then again, as in every area of life, consider what you really need, use up what you have and simplify!

When it comes to ingredients, I think a good place to start is shopping with companies that have certifications you can look up and understand, like organic, B corp, Fairtrade, carbon-neutral certifications and many others. No one certification is the answer to a perfect, 100 per cent healthy and no-waste product, but they're easy markers that a company or product is moving in the right direction. So read the packaging and see what the companies are saying, then do some research. If you want to research every ingredient you can absolutely do that. There are also websites where you can enter many products to see a general analysis of each and their ingredients.

Remember, as sustainability is becoming more fashionable, some companies will be marketing their product to make them look eco-friendly, but it might not be all it's cracked up to be. So it is important to put a little effort in here. Try to find friends or beauty bloggers who have gone on this journey already and can recommend some products to try.

TOILETRIES

The options for decreasing waste in this area are increasing by the day. Also, where before some products sacrificed a little of their effectiveness in order to be greener, that is increasingly no longer the case, which is exciting. Eco-friendly alternatives for soaps, deodorants, shampoos, conditioners, dry shampoos, shaving equipment, toothpastes and cotton pads, among other things, are all becoming more widely available in local shops or online.

Soap

If you don't want to buy a separate soap for hands, body and hair, liquid castile soap is a vegetable-based soap that isn't created with synthetic, petroleum-based or animal-based ingredients. It's a great multitasking option with simpler, more Earth-friendly, biodegradable and often safer ingredients for health. We use it as a shower gel, shampoo, hand soap and for so many other things, such as cleaning our home, spot-treating stains and even as laundry soap in a pinch.

Most of us are familiar with bar soap, which is often the cheapest way to go, but there's also the option to buy liquid soap in bulk, if you prefer it in that form.

66

Take a look at the ingredients, as well as the packaging, and think about the impact these might have on the planet.

99

Look for simple, more natural, organic ingredients and also ones that have a lower impact on the planet in both their creation and disposal. It's a great idea to opt for locally made soaps, too.

In order to avoid waste, it's important to care for your soap correctly. After each use, let it dry out properly by setting it on a well-draining soap dish, otherwise it can quickly turn to mush. Alternatively, collect an attractive pile of stones for the soap to sit on – it works just as well and means you don't have to purchase a new item!

If you have guests and want clean, new soap for them, try slicing a bar into pieces and just giving them a small slice rather than a full new bar. This is also a great tip for travelling, if you don't want to take a big bar around with you.

For liquid soaps, and to save buying dispensers over and over, invest in a glass soap dispenser or refill one that you already have, buying either in bulk or creating your own handwash by diluting liquid castile soap.

Deodorant

There are many options on the market that either come plastic-free, in a glass jar or are sold in compostable or paper packaging. Formulas and scents are getting better and there are many more ranges coming onto the market, meaning you can shop around and find the one that really works for you. You can also make your own, with many DIY recipes available on the internet with simple ingredients that can often be found in bulk.

Shampoo and conditioner

To avoid all those plastic bottles, shampoos and conditioners are now available in bar form from a lot of different companies. Some are definitely better than others, but there are plenty that are no different from washing and conditioning your hair with traditional bottle shampoo. They are even available for different hair types. As always, do a bit of research before buying.

Some people can be a bit confused as to how shampoo bars work – I was too at first! There are two ways: you can either lather it in your hands and then apply that lather to your hair or rub the bar directly onto your scalp. In my experience, lathering it directly onto your scalp is a much more workable method, but experiment and find what works for you.

You can also buy shampoo in bulk or in refillable metal containers if you want to reduce your plastic purchasing but not give up the liquid product.

Powdered dry shampoo is another option that can help people go longer in between washes, saving time, shampoo/conditioner and drying – not to mention water! There are many low-waste alternatives to the dry shampoos packaged in plastic and aerosol containers. It's also a fairly easy item to make yourself, using household items (see page 106) which are easy to buy in bulk and/or low-waste packaging.

DIY DRY SHAMPOO

Most homemade dry shampoos are a combination of cornflour or arrowroot with cinnamon, cocoa or other ingredients to achieve the right colour, and sometimes a few drops of essential oil for fragrance. You can adjust the proportions to be the correct colour for your hair, then shake it up in a jar and use a makeup brush to apply it. Dip the brush in the jar, tap it to get rid of any excess powder, brush it onto your roots and then through the hair. Use a regular brush to brush it through to finish.

Teeth

TOOTHBRUSHES

It's said that one billion toothbrushes are thrown into land-fill every year in the US alone, and they will all still be there in hundreds of years. There are many different ways to reduce waste when it comes to toothbrushes, particularly by opting for items made from more planet-friendly materials. The most common are bamboo toothbrushes – bamboo is a fast-growing, biodegradable, natural material, so these are a much more sustainable option. In compostable toothbrushes the bristles usually need to be removed with pliers before composting. You can also repurpose them before composting to use as a scrubbing brush for grout or small areas. Old toothbrushes are also useful as markers in your flower beds or pots, just remove the bristles, write on plant names and stick them in the soil.

Bamboo isn't the only option, recycled plastic options are also widely available, which can give more of the look that people are used to and also offer options for electric toothbrushes too.

TOOTHPASTE

Toothpaste tubes are not widely recyclable, but there are a few more eco-friendly options here as well. Toothpaste is widely available in a chewable tablet form – just crush them by biting and brush as normal. Pastes are also available in glass jars or tins rather than the hard-to-recycle tube. The alternatives feel different from the tube we are familiar with, but you quickly get used to them, don't worry! There are a few brands that create recyclable metal toothpaste tubes, and there are also companies that recycle some of the harder-to-recycle items like plastic toothpaste tubes, so if you do end up with one, you may be able to find a way to recycle it locally to you. As always, though, the best option is not to create that waste in the first place, if possible.

MOUTHWASH

Typically sold in plastic bottles, there are now brands that create mouthwashes in glass bottles to reduce plastics. These are often made with more natural ingredients, too. Try looking in a local or online low-waste store for different options. DIY mouthwash could be another way to go if you're up for a challenge, and there are many recipes for these online. Obviously, check with your dentist that as you reduce your waste your dental care plan is still looking good for your teeth!

FLOSS

Floss is typically made of synthetic fibres, but there are a few more easily broken-down options, too, such as bamboo and silk covered with beeswax or plant-based waxes. And there are better options for dental floss picks, too, which use plastic-free materials like wood or cornstarch.

Shaving

There are many options for lowering waste when it comes to shaving and hair removal. You can use a process called sugaring for a very low-waste home wax solution (this method melts down sugar to create a sticky caramel which you then use as wax), or you can invest in an epilator, which can remove hair over and over again with no extra apparatus (it does use energy, though).

For actual shaving, the most-used low-waste solution would be a reusable safety razor where you replace the blade and don't discard a whole razor each time. In most areas the metal blades can be stored and recycled, and with a little research you can find out how to do this in your local area. These have the added bonus of not having that small moisturizing/lubricating strip which can contain chemicals that help a shave but increase their carbon footprint – increasingly a lot of people now choose to avoid these because of health concerns associated with the chemicals they can contain.

To replace shaving cream, an unpackaged bar soap works well, so keep it simple with your regular bar soap choice, or look for one that is specifically designed for shaving.

As an alternative to a safety razor there are various options, such as disposable razors, that offer some level of recyclability or are made from already recycled materials. Over time the cost of these will probably add up to what you would spend on a reusable wooden razor, so I would try to avoid these if you can.

Makeup and haircare

The lowest-impact solution for makeup when it comes to human health and the environment is probably just to not wear any. For those of us who do still want to wear makeup, there are options that are kinder to the Earth that often have the added bonus of being those that are made from ingredients that are gentler on our bodies, too.

Makeup, hair care and all personal care products are an incredibly personal thing, and how you choose them varies hugely from person to person. There is, as in so many areas, no right answer and we have to come back to taking one step forward each time we're able to – maybe when we run out of a product or have time to research a switch.

"

To keep it simple, reducing the number of products you use and using them less is a potentially easier way to reduce your impact.

"

This removes the need to spend time researching brand practices or ingredients by simply slowing our consumption, which by default lowers our impact on the Earth.

There are also a number of simple one-ingredient ways to use products you may already have in your home for personal care, like apple cider vinegar as a facial toner and olive oil as a facial cleanser. You don't need to turn to your kitchen cabinet for your full routine, but if you can replace one thing with a simple, natural product you already own you can reduce the need to buy new products.

It can be overwhelming to switch makeup products when you have a favourite, and there are many factors to consider on its impact on the Earth, too. There's the creation of the packaging of the products and the secondary packaging of shipping if you don't buy it from a physical shop. There's the impact of shipping and of sourcing the ingredients, the effect they have on our bodies and the disposal of the packaging. Any of these, or other areas, are opportunities for a company to reduce its footprint, so look out for brands doing better on any of those. There are many certifications – from Leaping Bunny, to organic, to B corp – that speak to the sourcing, ingredients and testing of a product and other factors that I think are great things to look at when making choices.

Natural ingredients don't always mean a lower footprint and neither do plant-based ones, but both can mean a company is doing better in this area. When it comes to the environmental impact, I think you have to dig into the company and understand what they are committed to – again, looking for external certifications and researching what those are is a great way to learn more.

Also, if you find a company that looks good, don't be afraid to reach out to them in an email, phone call or via social media and ask questions or for them to point you in the direction of answers about their products. If they don't have the answers, that's a sign that they're likely not doing the things you'd want them to be!

I'd suggest visiting a shop that is focused on low-impact skincare and makeup as a way to find potential options grouped together already, so you're not shopping in the dark. Then you can sort through those to find the items that fit your values and your needs.

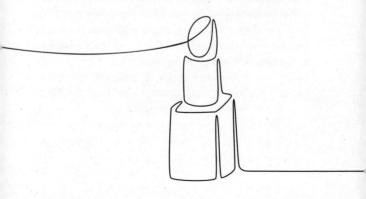

Period supplies

There are many different eco-friendly options available for period supplies, from disposables that have a lower footprint, to reusable versions of traditional disposables, to menstrual cups or absorbent, washable underwear. Initially, reusables are more expensive than disposables, but depending on how many you invest in, you can recoup the cost very quickly.

You need to find what works well for you and fits into your life. Reusables obviously need to be taken home if you are out, so a lower-footprint disposable might make more sense if you are always on the move. A cup doesn't need to be disposed of, simply emptied and replaced, but at certain times of life or for certain people a cup may not be the appropriate item (like post-partum). It's all about what is best for you, and that may be using a variety of methods at different moments.

For an easy way to clean reusables, take them into the shower with you to give them a first rinse, then throw them in the wash with your clothes. By the time they get to the wash they'll be mostly clean anyway. You can also throw them in a fast-rinse cycle then add them to a full wash, but I prefer the shower as it's using water that's already being used. Rather than tumble drying these, drying outdoors or in direct sunlight will help with bleaching them, if necessary, and reduce energy use, too. The UV rays of sunlight are also known to have antibacterial properties, which, along with fresh outside air, can help deodorise items as they dry too.

WATER USE

*If you have ever experienced a drought,
you may have had to learn to conserve water,
not so much out of being 'eco-friendly' as out
of necessity or external regulation.*

Water use is obviously a key area to talk about in the bathroom. From the shower to the bath, basin, toilet or even a bidet, each can be a source of water waste. Most people can probably halve their water use without feeling it too much. Set yourself a challenge! Can you halve the length of your shower even once a week? Or turn the water off while you lather up your soap or shampoo? Here are a few more ideas to reduce your water usage in the bathroom:

- Install a low-flow shower; based on the flow this could halve your water use without you needing to change the length of your shower.

- If you're installing a new toilet, look for a high-efficiency or low-flow one, or put a plastic bottle filled with water or a device made for this purpose in the tank, which will reduce the amount of water used on each flush.

- Check for a toilet leak and get it fixed if you have one – you can often see or hear a constant dripping, but alternatively if you put a few drops of food colouring in the top of the toilet (where the flushing mechanism is) it should only get into the toilet bowl when you flush. If it's leaking, you'll see it in the bowl without flushing the toilet.

- Make repairs quickly on anything else that's leaking.

- Cut down your time in the shower, even by a minute – each minute saves multiple gallons of water over time. Set yourself a timer for any amount less than your usual length of shower and see if you can reduce it.

- Opt for a short shower over a bath or run a shallower bath.

- Turn off the water or at least turn down the flow while you shampoo, condition, or shave to save water you don't need to use. Do the same when you are brushing your teeth.

- Try being a little less quick to flush the toilet and only flush when you really need to (see opposite).

- Use dry shampoo instead of washing your hair as regularly.

- Put a bucket in your shower to save the water that runs while it heats up – use it to water plants or pour it down the toilet – did you know that doing this will flush it?!

TOILET TALK

The toilet is a place where you can reduce your water wastage. You might need to get out of your comfort zone of what's normal to you, but this is a great opportunity to assess where our idea of 'normal' came from. To many, 'normality' has become a level of cleanliness and neat perfection that's really only possible in certain parts of the world and in recent years. Now, obviously, there are some huge advantages to developments in cleanliness that I'm not disputing here, but we need to address the fact that we might actually be flushing away more waste than we really need to.

One saying that's often quoted about saving water and toilet flushing is: 'If it's yellow, let it mellow, if it's brown, flush it down.' The idea being to leave liquid waste in the bowl, but flush solids. When I was pregnant (and using the toilet more frequently as a result), I became aware that I was often flushing away very little with a lot of water, and that it probably was unnecessary. We did have to have some family chats about what we were comfortable with in order to come to the right balance for our home, but my point is that we shouldn't shy away from chats like these. In fact, they are needed on this journey, very much so.

It really is
all about
questioning
what you're
used to, then
picking the
option that is
right for you
and your home.

Cistern displacement device

You can also reduce the amount of water used in each flush and still have an effective toilet. If you can access the water cistern of your toilet, you can simply add a device that will displace some of the water. That way, after each flush the cistern requires less water to refill, but will still contain enough water to produce an effective flush. Purpose-built devices are available to buy or are often available free on request from your local water authority or council, but it's also possible to make one at home. Fill a used plastic bottle with some small rocks or sand – enough to weigh it down – and seal tightly. Place it in the toilet cistern, well away from the refill mechanism.

Saving on toilet paper

If you want to reduce the amount of toilet paper you use, lots of people living a low-waste lifestyle swear by installing a bidet. If you don't have the ability to put one in your home, or don't want the upfront spend, that's ok. There are now more and more options for toilet paper that has a less negative footprint, these include versions that are manufactured using recycled materials, use fewer harmful chemicals, or are not wrapped in plastic. Cloths are another option that people turn to instead of disposable toilet paper, the idea being that they can be washed and reused over and over again. This may be scary sounding to a lot of people, but if you've ever used cloth nappies, suddenly it's a concept that is a lot more understandable and less crazy. It really is all about questioning what you're used to, then picking the option that is right for you and your home.

CLEANING THE BATHROOM

*I don't use any products in my bathroom
that are any different from the simple ones
I use in the rest of my home.*

White vinegar, water, bicarbonate of soda and liquid castile soap go a long way here. You really can keep it simple and you don't need to have a lot of different cleaners for different purposes. If you want specific toilet cleaners, bath cleaners and purchasable products for different areas I suggest finding options that you can buy in bulk from a local or online store, or finding a company that sells more environmentally friendly options – which are now widely available for most of the things we're used to using. Look for companies using recycled or recyclable or refillable packaging and no-fragrance or all-natural fragrances such as essential oils.

I use old cut-up T-shirts and purpose-made cotton or bamboo washable cleaning clothes, or old cloth nappy inserts for the majority of my bathroom cleaning. Then I keep a second all-purpose spray bottle for bathroom use, with the 50:50 vinegar and water mix in it and a few drops of liquid castile soap. If you have a porcelain bath or any kind of more delicate tile that might be harmed by vinegar, I'd suggest using just a bowl of warm water, castile soap and a sponge or rag, then rinsing well. For the toilet I use the same all-purpose spray, spraying lots in and letting it stand while I clean something else, then I scrub it with the toilet brush and flush. You can also sprinkle on bicarbonate of soda after the vinegar, which will fizz and then you can just scrub it in the same way.

Old toothbrushes come in really handy for cleaning grout and small corners of the bathroom, so I recommend saving and labelling those as old to give them a second life. You can also invest in a wooden toilet brush when you next need a new one – there's no reason to switch out one you already have, just take good care of it so it lasts, but if and when you need a new one, choose a wooden one as there are many options that are now plastic-free. When you're done cleaning the toilet, pour some vinegar over the brush to rinse and clean it, then let it sit between the toilet and the seat to dry fully. You can also soak the brush and holder in a half-and-half solution of white vinegar and water overnight then rinse with hot water and air dry.

Bathrooms are another great space where you can add plants to your home. Placing eucalyptus leaves in the shower is a popular way to freshen up the bathroom, and the natural oils from the plant will release, which can help to open up your nasal passageways.

BEDROOM

CHAPTER 5

SLEEPING

Many people initially approach choosing their mattress and bedding from a health perspective, but it's also worth looking at your sleeping arrangements from the point of view of creating a lower environmental footprint.

Mattress

A key consideration for mattresses is what to do with it when it reaches the end of its life. Look at whether your mattress has been made to last for a long time and how, when it needs disposing of, its component parts are going to impact the planet. In particular, look at natural-fibre options as much as possible, be they cotton, wool or natural rubber. Some mattresses are now fully recyclable, so again, do your research about how to dispose of it before you buy, even if you are ten years ahead of yourself.

Bed frame

There are many types of bed frame available, but I prefer simpler wooden ones, taking into consideration the sourcing of the wood and the stains and paints used, and thinking about their impact on the planet. As always, consider buying second-hand before you look at new options. If you are varnishing your bed frame, use your own stain of steel wool and vinegar and apply some beeswax or a natural oil to finish. If you do want to paint it, buy an eco-friendly paint.

Bed linen

Some people don't like the idea of second-hand bed linen, so if that's you, there are eco-friendly ways of buying new. Always choose natural fibres such as bamboo or cotton over synthetics, which are less impactful on the environment but will also be more breathable. If you do go for cotton sheets, choose organic and sustainably grown cotton. As always, you'll need to pick what makes sense for your budget but it can save you money in the long run to invest in better quality bed linen, as it will last much longer.

WARDROBE

Build a capsule wardrobe

A capsule wardrobe is essentially a smaller-than-average set of clothes containing a minimal number of pieces that are designed to work well together and be worn for longer, in rotation. The intention is to simplify your life, making decisions easier and reducing unnecessary shopping. There are many tutorials available online on how to put one together; go with whatever works for you, but a small capsule wardrobe that changes seasonally (usually created from what you already own) keeps things simple and saves the cost of buying lots of new things from season to season. It also means that each piece is carefully chosen with the intention of wearing it and pairing it with other things, which leads to fewer impulse buys. It might take some initial outlay and then sporadic additions, but if you can find a combination of clothes that can be stored and rotated from season to season, this will be a big waste saver.

The intention is to simplify your life, making decisions easier and reducing unnecessary shopping.

99

How to shop second-hand

When I buy second-hand clothing, I'm happy to be buying clothes that are already in circulation, but I'm still looking for certain things. I try to find quality pieces that are the best made and that will last me through the seasons. I'm also looking for pieces made from natural materials, such as wool and cotton. Well-made clothes tend to be easier to repair when they finally do wear out, and natural fibres don't contribute microplastics to the waste stream during washing. When clothes finally reach the end of their life with me, if I really can't pass them on, natural fibres are more repurposable.

How to shop for new items

As a hugely generalised rule, when it comes to sustainability, ethical practices and the environment, I treat clothing companies as 'guilty' until proven innocent or at least better. Yes, there will be times when this doesn't hold up, but with more demand than ever for transparency on production and the environment, companies that really are making steps forward are quick to talk about it. If a company stays quiet about what positive steps they're taking, they're likely not doing very much. Send an email or call customer services and ask some questions and you'll quickly find out a bit about their environmental practices.

Be aware of 'greenwashing', which is when a company conveys a false impression that they are doing more good than they are. If clothing companies use terms like 'eco' or 'sustainable', dig into what they really mean by that and judge for yourself whether their claims hold.

When I buy brand new, I'm looking for the same qualities as when I shop second-hand, but with even more thought to the impact on the Earth of its creation.

Clothing swap events or jumble sales

Sometimes called 'swishing', clothes swaps are becoming more popular. There are many ways to host events like this, but clothing swaps and jumble sales can be a great way to give clothes new lives. You can get together with friends or join up with local groups online to organise a swap.

Alternatively, host a garage or jumble sale, and have everyone price their own pieces. You could then shop from each other or invite locals to come and shop (mark the hangers with the initials of the seller and note at a single paypoint how much goes to each person). Another way to do this is to have people donate items and all proceeds from the sale go to charity. Paying people directly for their clothing makes it easier for them to part with pieces they don't wear but might be holding on to due to perceived value.

If you don't feel as though you have good second-hand resources in your area, this can be a good way to start, with the added bonus that you get people thinking about the need to clear out and swap, not shop!

Don't think
people will
think less of
you if you
aren't in a new
outfit every
time they
see you.

ORGANISING A
CLOTHES SWAP

There's no right way to do a clothes swap but you want to make sure the set-up is clear and everything is arranged so that everyone knows what is going on. How many people are coming will change how you run the event, but you need to pick a venue that will be good for the number of guests you're inviting and the amount of items you're suggesting they each bring. If you can have racks for hanging items that will really help with display, but you can also lay them on tables.

Decide how many items you want people to bring and the parameters – are accessories wanted? Shoes? Or just garments? Communicate that you are looking for things that are in good condition, clean, high quality and on a hanger (if you need that). You can allow people to bring as many items as they want or you can specify a certain number – this will mean people show up with an amount that will create a good swap, but also won't give you bags and bags of clothes to manage at the event.

If you're doing a smaller event with friends you may just all look at the clothes and do an informal swap, but if you have a bigger group you can create a system where people get a ticket for every item they bring which they can then exchange for other items, 'paying' with the tickets. However, it's also important to communicate that this event isn't about exact values, it's about the heart of swapping and revamping your wardrobe without buying new. Setting expectations and having everyone bring quality items is helpful. With a larger event you can have someone on the door vetting items so that everything is of a similar quality.

Think about sizing and potentially include some non-sized items – you could request that everyone brings one thing that's an accessory or one-size-fits-all, then also make sure you invite a range of dress sizes with multiple people at a similar size (especially at a smaller event) if you can so that there is good potential for swapping.

Set up well-labelled sections so that items are grouped together for easy shopping – and if you are assigning different ticket values to different items, have a way to mark hangers accordingly. If you have a larger number of people attending you may need set-up time after people have arrived.

Have a plan for what you will do with the leftover clothes at the end and communicate to people where they will go. Find a local charity, shelter or organisation that will take the clothes and use them well. If you have storage and plan to make this a regular event you could keep some pieces to start the collection for swapping at your next event.

Rent or borrow

For special occasions, rather than buying an outfit you are unlikely to wear again or for a very long time, try borrowing an outfit from a friend or using a local or online outfit rental service.

Rewear

I love seeing celebrities rewear clothes for events. Kate Middleton, Emma Watson and Cate Blanchett are all celebrity names who do this regularly. They've rejected the idea that we should wear different or new things all the time. Nowadays, there's too much worry about what we last wore in public and that we should make sure we don't choose the same thing next time. It means that the average piece of clothing gets worn such a small number of times that it's incredibly wasteful. We should have more confidence in our own decisions. Don't think people will think less of you if you aren't in a new outfit every time they see you. I wore the same jumpsuit to every formal event throughout the last summer season and I embraced it! Use what you have and rewear your clothing for as long as it's serviceable.

ONLINE RESELLING
- A CAVEAT

There are increasing ways of finding second-hand pieces online. There is a growing trade in buying and reselling second-hand clothing that I think is actually fuelling those who subscribe to 'fast fashion' (the buying of multiple poorly made pieces at a low price and changing clothes very often).

Personally, I would always try to buy first from charity shops. When people donate unwanted clothing to a charity shop they are not profiting from it and therefore you are less likely to be fuelling a shopping habit. Children's clothes are a slight exception here: given the speed that they outgrow pieces, reselling the clothes online to give them a second or third life, or even more, makes sense.

LAUNDRY

Washing

Washing your clothes on the coldest wash possible removes some need for heating water, which saves energy, but it also helps clothes keep their original colour and shape, extending their lifespan. It can also help with wrinkles, so this might save you both time and energy in ironing, too.

Make sure you have a full load of laundry so that you're maximising cleaning for the water and energy used in each cycle. It can be tempting to throw a few items in in a pinch, but planning well, spot cleaning and airing where you can and making a habit of only washing full loads can help you reduce energy wastage. At the same time, don't be tempted to overstuff a load and reduce the cleaning efficiency.

Know your washer, your detergent, your clothes and your water. Depending on where you are and your water type, what you're washing, your machine and your detergent, you'll need to adjust the factors for the wash. In general, you want to use the lowest temperature and the least detergent possible for each wash. If you have soft-water areas you'll generally need less detergent, and if what you're washing is only very lightly soiled you may be able to go without detergent every now and again.

Drying

When it comes to drying, skip the tumble dryer! If you can – and most of us can – hang clothes on a line outside or on a drying rack, or even over items around the house – whatever works for your space. Obviously, if you're washing at a laundromat, it is harder to lug home a wet bag of clothes, but if you have the space to air-dry inside or outside, do it!

"

Even if you only air-dry certain items, such as the ones that dry fastest, every little helps.

"

If you are using a dryer and you tend to reach for dryer sheets, natural wool balls can be a great alternative to the dryer sheets that contribute to landfill but also have additional ingredients and scents. They can be used as is, or you can put a few drops of essential oils, such as lavender, on them to naturally scent a load.

If you use the dryer for fluffiness, you can shake the clothes before putting them on the line, which may help a bit. Detergent residue plays into the stiffness of clothes, so try reducing the amount of detergent you use or throwing half a cup of distilled white vinegar into the final load of your laundry rinse cycle or the fabric softener drawer.

You can also throw the clothes in the drier at the end of line or rack drying for just a few minutes with wool balls and natural essential oil scents to fluff and scent the laundry.

I'd also recommend doing a washing and drying audit in the same way I recommend a rubbish bin audit. Look at the clothes and items you're putting in the wash and what's going in the dryer.

What's being washed and why? Is there any way you could stop any of those items from needing the wash? Are there lots of kids' play clothes that you could wash less regularly and just dress them in messy play clothes a few days in a row? Are there lots of clothes with marks from cooking – could you make a point of wearing an apron? Are there kids' clothes soiled with food too often – could you get a full bib with sleeves or feed them without clothes?! Are you washing a lot of items for ease that really have one tiny mark – could you spot clean instead? Do you wash things that aren't marked but just need freshening up – could anything be hung and aired for freshness instead? And on drying, are you needing to use the dryer from lack of planning, unnecessary ease or simply habit? That can be where a lot of dryer use comes from in homes. Make a plan for how you can hang clothes and invest in a washing line or drying rack. They aren't expensive and will pay for themselves fairly quickly if you are a regular dryer user. Creating a plan for a new way of doing something is often a large part of what's needed to change habits and change the amount of waste we create!

Messy or house clothes

As someone at home with kids, I've implemented 'messy clothes'. When we're around the house or playing outside, we don't put on clean clothes every day. We have a house outfit that we wear for a good few days before we wash it. When we go out, we change, then when we're back at home, we put on our messy clothes again. It saves a LOT of laundry.

Also, use an apron. If you're in the kitchen or doing other messy tasks, throw on an apron to save your clothes. You usually don't have to wash an apron after every use, so this does reduce the amount of laundry you'll create.

Spot clean

As soon as little spills or marks happen, take the time to deal with them, if you can. Then at the end of the day spot clean any lightly soiled items and hang them up to dry overnight, rather than washing the whole item every time. This saves water (depending on how careful you are as you spot clean) and energy. It has the added benefit of improving the life of your clothes, as washing them too often can damage the fibres.

Some small marks can be removed with a fingernail or palette knife after they've dried by just gently scratching or brushing off a residue, liquids can first be carefully blotted out onto a rag. Then using water – or the appropriate cleaner for the item – white vinegar or castile soap, treat the area and rinse out. If you can't get the mark out fully, the pre-treating will help once you put it into the wash.

Plastic microfibres can enter the water stream as we do laundry and end up in drinking water, fish and sea salt.

Just don't dry the area with heat if the mark isn't removed or it may be harder to get rid of later. It's amazing how many things don't need to be washed if they are taken care of then spot treated as needed. Drying whites in the sun after spot cleaning will help, too – lay the item flat in full sun to dry and it will help to lift any marks left after cleaning.

Guppy bags

If you're washing synthetic fibres such as acrylic, nylon and polyester, try to wash them as little as possible (which I recommend for all clothes, to help extend their life), but you could also look at using a 'guppy bag'. These are bags that you can put your clothes into to reduce fibre breakage and catch any synthetic microfibres that are released, stopping them from entering and polluting the water during the washing cycle. The tiny microfibres are instead collected in the guppy bag and can then be placed into another closed item you're already disposing of to keep them contained, then put directly into the rubbish bin.

If not disposed of properly, plastic microfibres can enter the water stream as we do laundry and end up in waterways and then drinking water, fish and sea salt, to name a few places. Being made of plastic, these do not degrade. Microfibres are an issue outside of laundry and are released in many ways by the degradation of waste plastic, worn plastic-based clothing and washing synthetic fibres, but washing clothes is thought to contribute a large percentage of the plastic microfibre pollution.

MENDING

Nowadays, the ability to sew and repair clothing is something that few people know how to do or even make time for.

We've all heard of that wartime slogan 'make do and mend', but it's definitely not the slogan ringing in most people's ears when they think about clothing. 'Buy new and spend' would probably be a more accurate version of what we are taught to think by advertising and fashion culture. What that means is that items with very little wrong with them get thrown out, and not even directed towards other people for resale or gifting. Even if they aren't thrown away, we often just stop wearing those pieces of clothing, adding to the feeling of need for new items.

"

With just a little work, though,
so many small fixes can be made.

"

It's also something I'm thinking about when I'm buying new or second-hand clothes: 'how easy will this be to repair?'

Knitted wool sweaters, socks and denim are easy to learn to repair yourself. There are also several brands, particularly denim brands, that offer free repairs on their products, so keep an eye out for those offers as you're purchasing! If you don't buy an item with repairs included and you don't want to be the one to do the mending, consider outsourcing the mending to someone else over throwing out the item. Look locally for sewing repairs and alterations services. It doesn't have to be too time-consuming to do it yourself, though – learn how to repair the problem and then, next time you are watching TV, grab the item and take the time to do a little mending.

Invest in a simple sewing kit: a needle, some pins and a few colours of thread are all you need to make a start. That way, when something breaks, you'll be all set up to grab a few minutes, whenever you have them, to actually mend those items.

If you wear tights often, you might want to add nail polish to your mending kit to run around the edge of a hole or ladder, as this is the best way to preserve tights for longer wear. If something is beyond repair I often keep any parts or it that could be used to patch another item or cut it up for kitchen rags or cleaning, save it for stuffing or wrapping, use it for kids' crafts or put it in textile recycling.

Different techniques can be used for different items, and I'd recommend looking online for videos that can help you with your specific item, but below I'm going to cover darning because I think it's a great place to start. This method can be used on lots of clothing, but start with socks, which are a lower-stakes item on which to practise!

DARNING

Darning socks (or another clothing item) involves weaving a thread back and forth over a thinned part or hole in an item to close a gap and reinforce the area. It's something I was taught to do as a child and I'm glad not only that I learned to do it but that my parents showed me that there was value in repairing old rather than just buying new. Learning these skills may involve an initial time investment but it's about valuing materials and the items we bring into our homes and taking care of them to give them the longest life possible. And that makes these things worth learning!

YOU'LL NEED:

- The sock or item to be darned, preferably at the first moment you see a hole or even just when you see thinning so you can reinforce it before it goes through.

- Thread of a similar weight and colour to that of the item you're darning – but you can also use a contrasting colour if you want to see the darned spot, or if it's more practical to use what you have and not buy multiple colours for different items.

- A needle that will fit the thickness of thread.

- A darning egg to go inside the sock as you sew, but you can absolutely do it without one of these: a lightbulb or a solid ball can do the same thing.

At one end or corner of the area you want to darn, start sewing a running stitch – basically going up and down through the fabric so you see dashes across the material - - - - - - -. If you are repairing a hole, you want to imagine a patch around it so that the darned area is about double the size of the hole. Even though you'll be darning a perfectly good area, it will create the strength of the threads to cover the hole.

Do the running stitch going through the sock up and down with your needle until you have little dashes across the area, then turn it around and do the same thing parallel coming back the other way. The closer you can get to the second row, the stronger the patch will be. Then just keep going up and down with the running stich the whole way across the area. When you get to the other side, do the same thing at 90 degrees to your initial rows, going in and out of the threads to create a weave over the hole that patches it strongly and fully. You can knot the beginning and the end if you want to, but in a sock it can create a bump that's not comfortable to wear. As you're doing a fine running stitch and weaving it, the stitches should be secure without a knot, but add one if you want to.

You can also darn jumpers or other pieces of clothing, and this method works well for denim with a piece of fabric secured behind the hole. Pin it in place, then just do the same thing!

LIFE
ADMIN

CHAPTER 6

SAVING ENERGY

It's easy to have a lot of things plugged in at home, which are all using energy even when they're not in use.

Remember to regularly turn things off or unplug them when they are not in use. Write a little list of appliances and light switches to check you've turned off before bed or before leaving the house to remind you, until it's second nature!

Some of these have been covered already but here's a quick list of the things you can do to reduce your energy use in your home:

- **Use lower-energy appliances or don't use appliances at all**, for example washing dishes by hand or air-drying instead of tumble drying.

- **Replace lightbulbs with energy efficient ones.**

- **Install energy efficient windows** (if your windows need replacing anyway), or increase the insulation around them if you live in an old house and have draughty windows.

- **Switch to a green energy supplier.**

- **Consider an energy-usage monitor** so you can see where your energy is being used and assess if there are any savings you can make.

- **Turn off all appliances when you are not using them** instead of leaving them on standby.

- **Assess whether you need to heat your house as much as you do or whether you could simply wear more clothes indoors.**

- **Install a smart thermostat** which makes heating more efficient by only heating the rooms you are using.

- **Wash clothes at the lowest temperature possible.**

- **Seal cracks in floors and skirting boards to reduce draughts** to ensure you are not wasting energy on heating that is escaping outside.

HOME
OFFICE

Paper, printing and pens

If you look in the bin of a home office, you'd see that paper is probably the thing that gets tossed in most often. Think about what you are choosing to print before you print it. Does it really need to be printed or could it be viewed and shared digitally just as easily? Make sure you are recycling your paper, not just binning it. Look at sourcing recycled paper and greener printer ink, too.

When you are printing, make sure you print on both sides of the paper, and save any used paper to write notes on. Shredded paper cannot always be recycled but it can be composted.

If you haven't invested in a fountain pen and jar of ink, try it. It's an adjustment, but it becomes an easy swap after a while. That way, you never need to buy another pen!

Electrical goods

Electrical goods are a complex topic, especially when it comes to the disposal or recycling of electronic waste. And we need to apply our thinking to electrical equipment used elsewhere in the home – not just the office.

The first thing is to consider what you're purchasing. There are more and more electrical gadgets available nowadays, which can be used throughout the home, and it's easy to think they are important and necessary. But, before we buy, we should take a moment to think about whether we truly need them.

Rather than buying new, consider the option of buying second-hand. In an area where people are buying new products all the time, there are often a lot of perfectly usable products that are being disposed of that could last for many years to come.

66

Take care of the items you do have
so that you can use them for as long
as possible.

99

It can be tempting to just buy new products when old ones go wrong, especially when it is cheaper than the cost of repairing them, but we have to remember that 'cheaper' is only taking one side of the story into account. Think about the environmental cost of throwing something away that could be repaired and reused.

❝

We should be thinking in terms of
scaling back what we believe we need,
taking care of items and repairing
them well to give them as long a life
as possible.

❞

Then, when they really have reached the end of their useful life, disposing of them correctly. This is particularly important with electrical goods as they often contain many potentially toxic components. Contact your local authority or look online on your local authority or recycling website to see how you should dispose of these things in your area. There are services in some areas that will collect and properly recycle or dispose of electrical goods. You can also contact local non-profits to see if they take donations of what you need to get rid of, sometimes they will accept certain used electronics.

The home office is also a place where lots of electrical goods are likely to be plugged in, so make sure you're using them minimally and turning things off when you leave the room.

MAIL

Looking at what enters your home through the front door and being stringent about it will help you reduce your waste and develop systems that lead to being less wasteful throughout the home.

Go paperless

A lot of companies that traditionally sent paper mail now give customers the option to go paperless and receive information online. This can be a great option for reducing your paper waste. While there is a carbon footprint associated with emails, they don't produce rubbish in the home, and the footprint is likely much smaller than that created by printing, posting and potentially returning the same content in paper form.

While the email footprint is small, it's worth remembering that most of us send and receive many more emails each week than we would have received as items of paper post, so in general – with both paper post and emails – try to keep it minimal. Unsubscribe from anything you can in any format and, especially where lots of mail is sent, go paperless if you can.

Circulars and junk mail

Reduce the amount of unwanted mail you receive by putting a sign on your door to deter leafleters. Depending on where you live, there are also ways to remove your name from groups that contribute to junk mail. Contact your local postal service or look online for options in your neighbourhood.

Reuse / repurpose / recycle

First, if it's something you need to unsubscribe from, take a moment to do it as soon as something comes through from the company, or batch up the mail for a week and set some time aside to do multiple real post and email subscription cancellations all at once.

Next, make sure you're reusing/repurposing/recycling the items as well as possible.

Reuse should be the first to go: can the envelope, postal box or parcel wrapping be used again for sending something else? I always slice open envelopes and packages, rather than ripping them, so that I can save them for reuse. You can put a label or a piece of paper over the old address. Consider whether pieces of paper can be used again for writing a shopping list or to make random notes. Newspaper can be used to line a rubbish or compost bin or can be used to make biodegradable plant pots. Card can be used at the base of a compost bin for easy emptying. Always try to think of a way in which things could be creatively reused.

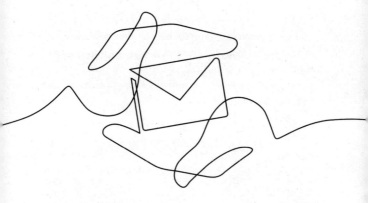

After reusing, and if you have the facility, take a look to see if the item is compostable. More and more circulars and mailouts are being created to be biodegradable, in which case, dispose of these as needed.

Beyond that, recycling is a great option. You may need to pull envelopes apart to separate the little plastic windows from the paper, or remove magazines from plastic covers. As always, you need to check with your local authority to see what recycling can be accepted. If something isn't an option for kerbside recycling, sometimes there are local facilities you can take your items to for wider recycling options.

GIFTING

I'll be honest, eco-gifting can feel difficult at first, especially if you're working within a budget.

People have an idea of what can be purchased with a certain amount of money and that usually doesn't account for things being made in an eco-friendly, local or lower-impact way, which is usually more costly. Gifting is also one of those issues where being short on time and needing something quickly often leads to unnecessary impact, as we lean on quick shipping from places that don't always have the best environmental or ethical credentials, items packaged in ways we wouldn't choose and delivered by faster methods that often have a higher footprint. It's one of the places I've really had to learn to think differently and be smart.

I now keep a 'gift drawer' and it has been a game changer when it comes to keeping gifts eco-friendly and lower impact. In it, I keep small gifts that I can use for multiple things, like dinner gifts or to slip in with a birthday card, such as bars of paper-wrapped, Fairtrade organic chocolate, bottles of wine, or small things I've found at random times that I know will come in useful later. Be mindful of shopping ahead too much, though – if what you buy won't get used, ultimately it's more wasteful. I keep some larger gifts, too, especially ones that are universally suitable for many people. It lets me shop in the sales and stock up on pieces when I find deals or useful items.

> I've also just had to get over the worry of being different from other people and celebrate the good in homemade gifts.
>
> I give different kinds of gifts, I own that and it's more than ok.

I'd rather do that and stay true to my values of creating less waste than buying more and more 'stuff' every time I need a gift. It's also often more thoughtful to give someone something personal and homemade that you've put time into.

Are you growing tomatoes from seed? Grow a few extra so you'll have little tomato plants to give in the coming weeks and months. Are you making granola? Look ahead to the week, and if you need a gift to take somewhere, double the recipe! Plan bread-baking for a day when you need a gift and bake an extra loaf. You can get more and more creative depending on your skills, maybe you can sew and you could give someone a beautifully handmade purse, maybe you have kids and get them involved? Work with what you have skills-wise and item-wise, and if you want lots of ideas for creative homemade presents, maybe jump on Pinterest and get some inspiration.

IDEAS FOR
HOMEMADE GIFTS

- A loaf of bread (include some of your sourdough starter or maybe a tea towel or fabric tote bag to wrap it in that can be kept)

- A jar of granola

- A seedling or plant

- A thoughtful card with a gift voucher or money

- Homemade vanilla extract

- A homemade gift certificate for services like date-night babysitting, cooking a meal, or anything else you can offer to help

- A baked good like a tray of brownies or a jar of biscuits – you could gift them in a second-hand pan or dish that could be kept. I keep my eye out any time I'm in a charity shop for items like this that I can fill and turn into a gift

- A jar of homemade nut butter

- A bag of coffee with second-hand sourced coffee mugs or a French press

- A drawing or piece of art by you

- A second-hand book that makes you think of the person you are gifting to with a note inside and wrapped in a saved ribbon or string

- A homemade body scrub, body butter, bath bomb or other self-care item

- A jar of homemade dry shampoo (see page 106)

Another idea is to give people services or experiences. It can be a great way to go for something meaningful that's free from waste. Someone once gifted me the time and resources of putting together a compost setup for my garden. It was THE best gift. You could also gift someone a meal out with you or a trip. This can be tailored to price and person.

"

> Keep a list of bookmarked websites or stores with eco options where you can get gifts.

"

In terms of requesting gifts, one easy route to go down is a 'no gifts please' policy. Alternatively, request money to put towards an experience, or guide friends and family to a specific wish list or list of stores explaining your values, if appropriate. For our son's last birthday party, I suggested people regifted a toy or book from their home that they were done with, but also added that no gifts were needed.

GIFT WRAPPING

It's a great idea to keep a box of strings and ribbons for wrapping gifts – it's amazing how quickly they can accumulate! Keep the string from veggie boxes or parcel wrappings. Keep the wrapping paper and ribbons from gifts you've received to use again. A lot of wrapping papers aren't actually recyclable (if you're buying new, check before you buy), but if it comes into your home, keep it for reuse to give it a second life. And keep an eye out for other materials that can be used as wrapping. A brown paper bag, cut up, can actually make gorgeous gift wrapping – simply add a great ribbon and maybe a sprig of greenery, a dried orange slice, a cinnamon stick or anything else you've saved to reuse. Once you set aside a small space to put away things for wrapping, you'll be amazed to see what you start to see as 'reusable' wrapping or decorating options. If you want to buy new for wrapping, my choice is a roll of recyclable brown paper because it has so many uses and can be styled in so many ways. There are also companies online that sell pretty recyclable, recycled or compostable wrapping papers, so those are what I'd reach for if I wanted something new beyond brown paper.

ON-THE-GO
KIT

*Most of us don't spend all day in
our homes. Preparing to leave is such
an important part of saving waste
when we're out and about.*

You can plan on the fly each time, or you can keep an
on-the-go kit in the kitchen or by the door so you can just
grab it and go. If you often travel by car, consider keeping
a similar kit in your car.

Here are some things you might like to include:

- **Reusable bags** There are many kinds of reusable bags
  you might have or want to carry with you, I use a thin
  cotton shoulder tote for carrying my to-go items and
  usually have a fabric drawstring bag inside, too, for
  taking home food that I've purchased (especially at
  bulk-shopping facilities), for collecting orange peels or
  other compostable items to take home, or to contain
  used napkins. A net bag is another great option that's
  tiny and light to carry empty but strong and versatile
  and can hold a large volume of produce, shopping or
  other items. Silicon bags are great for fully sealing items
  that need to be kept fresh or contained, or messier food
  items or things that might be wet like wipes (have a
  clean and a dirty bag). You can adjust what you throw
  in your to-go kit depending on your life and the outing.

When I'm leaving the house with kids, I always throw in extra silicon and drawstring bags for leftovers, small clothes and other needs that I know will crop up!

- **Coffee cup** This is probably the most commonly carried on-the-go item. Yet I ask myself how many people ever find themselves in a situation where a disposable coffee cup is truly unavoidable. For that reason, I decided that if I couldn't put my drink in a real cup (either from home or a reusable to-go mug), I would always say no to coffee. It makes me really check twice that I have a coffee cup with me!

- **Cloth napkins** These can be used for so many things, but disposable paper napkins are such a commonly accepted piece of waste. You don't need pricey ones – an old T-shirt or shirt can be cut up to make a great stash of 5–10 napkins. If you want to hem them around the edges, you can, but it's not essential. The thinness of T-shirt material means they are a very lightweight extra to your bag. After use, simply take them home again and throw them in with your laundry.

- **Reusable straw** It's probably easier to just say no to a straw (even a paper one) than to bring your own reusable. However, if you're someone who needs one to drink, then add one to your kit.

- **Cutlery or spork** If you're taking food to go, or buying it on the go, you'll likely need utensils to eat it with. You can get wooden or compostable cutlery and they may feel easier to grab, but I would always try to avoid that use of resources and bring my own regular cutlery. If you're limited on space, look at using a spork, but really a regular spoon or fork from home usually works.

- **Tiffin tin** If you're getting food while you're out and about, this is a really helpful item. Use a tiffin tin to contain items bought from food trucks, delis or supermarket counters, or use them to bring home leftovers after a restaurant meal rather than accepting a doggy bag or box.

- **Water bottle** Along with a coffee cup, this is probably one of the most useful items you can pack.

- **Handkerchief** Especially in winter, avoid using all those tissues and just create then carry a set of hankies for yourself.

- **Bag for dirty items** A fully sealable silicone bag is my top choice for this.

- **Mason jar** Great in the summer for iced coffee, smoothies, smoothie bowls, berries from the farmers' market, or soup leftovers from a restaurant, this is a flexible container for so many things.

CONCLUSION

THE POWER OF
SAYING 'NO'

Saying 'no' is completely free and it might be one of the biggest things you can do to change the amount of waste you create.

From refusing plastic cutlery to saying you don't need a printed receipt, we are often offered or just given a lot of things we don't actually need. But, despite it being such a short, two-letter word, it's something we can find really hard to say.

Often, people assume that if something's free then of course you'd want it. Who doesn't want free water? A free smoothie? A coffee in a paper cup when someone is grabbing a round for the office? Who wants to ask in a cocktail bar if it comes with a straw? But sometimes we need to ask ourselves whether we actually need something to establish whether we could say no. Or we have to pre-empt those free offers. Whenever I order food, especially at takeaway outlets, I'll first ask 'Does that come with any plastic or paper products?'. That way, I have the option of turning them down. If you don't want gifts at a birthday, make sure you make it clear to everyone beforehand. Learning how and where to say no can really help you reduce unnecessary waste.

AFFIRMATIONS AND DECLARATIONS

So many of the things we've discussed in this book are in part addressed or made consistent by changing the way we look at life and believing in the journey. I think it can be a game changer to take control of our own personal narrative on the changes we are making in our lives and make sure we are aligning our thoughts with the life we want to lead! This is especially so when, much as the world is changing to make this lifestyle more normal, we will often find ourselves being the odd one out or making choices that aren't in line with what the 'crowd' is doing.

66

It can be hard to carve out our own path when people around us are doing something so different.

99

So I think it's helpful to have some truths to come back to that keep us grounded and in the game. Having reminders like the ones below to read through every now and again, or one particular one to write out and put on the wall or fridge or front door can really keep us encouraged.

- My choices matter. They affect people beyond myself and I love that.

- I live by my beliefs. If I don't look like other people, that's ok – I'm pioneering what I believe in.

- Small changes make a difference. They lead on to more small changes and new life systems.

- I love the things that I have now. Not constantly buying more is a powerful way to live.

- Second-hand is beautiful. The beauty of creating a smaller and more positive footprint is real and I value it.

- My convenience is not at the expense of others. I'm happy to have to work harder to impact others less negatively.

- I invest my money carefully. I make sure that the things I bring into my home have taken and will take care of both people and the planet.

- My resources look different from those of other people. Rather than comparing myself to others, I use my time, energy, abilities and money to do what I can.

- It's ok to go without. There's a reason behind the things I choose not to have and I believe in it.

- It's ok to be misunderstood. I'm living the way I believe is best for the planet.

Remember:

- There's no 'one-size-fits-all' approach; moving forward is what counts.

- You can't tackle everything in the world, but you can make changes to the things you do.

- Where's the easiest place for you to start? Or the cheapest? Or the place that seems like it has the biggest impact? Pick something today, because starting is what really counts.

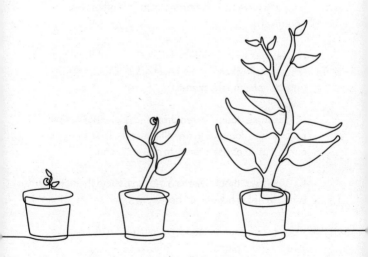

There's no 'one-size-fits-all' approach; moving forward is what counts.

INDEX

Ebury Press, an imprint of Ebury Publishing,
20 Vauxhall Bridge Road,
London, SW1V 2SA

Ebury Press is part of the Penguin Random House group of companies
whose addresses can be found at global.penguinrandomhouse.com

Penguin
Random House
UK

Text © Kezia Neusch 2020
Images © Shutterstock

First published by Ebury Press in 2020
www.penguin.co.uk

A CIP catalogue record for this book is available from the British Library

Design: Louise Evans

ISBN: 978-1-529-10781-4

Printed and bound in Great Britain by Clays Ltd, Elcograf S.p.A.

Penguin Random House is committed to a sustainable future for
our business, our readers and our planet. This book is made from
Forest Stewardship Council® certified paper.